I0106093

Atlantic Council
SCOWCROFT CENTER
FOR STRATEGY AND SECURITY

ICNC
International Center on
Nonviolent Conflict

Fostering a Fourth Democratic Wave:

A PLAYBOOK FOR COUNTERING THE AUTHORITARIAN THREAT

by Hardy Merriman, Patrick Quirk, and Ash Jain

Table of Contents

TASK FORCE FOR FOSTERING A FOURTH DEMOCRATIC WAVE

The authors would like to thank the members of the task force listed below for their input and contributions to the playbook. The views expressed in this playbook represent those solely of the authors and do not necessarily reflect the views or endorsement of the members of the task force.

Helena Bjuremalm
Swedish International Development
Cooperation Agency (Sida)

Admiral Dennis Blair (ret.)
University of North Carolina Chapel Hill

Esther Brimmer
Atlantic Council Board of Directors

Kizito Byenkya
Open Society Foundations

Kevin Casas-Zamora
International Institute for Democracy
and Electoral Assistance

Larry Diamond
Freeman Spogli Institute and Hoover Institution,
Stanford University

Ambassador Paula Dobriansky
Scowcroft Center for Strategy
and Security, Atlantic Council

Melanie Greenberg
Humanity United

Maina Kiai
Human Rights Watch

Leopoldo López
World Liberty Congress

Kristin Lord
International Research &
Exchanges Board (IREX)

Ivan Marovic
International Center on
Nonviolent Conflict (ICNC)

Derek Mitchell
(Task force co-chair)
National Democratic Institute (NDI)

Jonas Parello-Plesner
Alliance of Democracies Foundation

Lisbeth Pilegaard
(Task force co-chair)
European Endowment for Democracy (EED)
Danish Institute for Parties and Democracy (DIPD)

Doug Rutzen
International Center for
Not-for-Profit Law (ICNL)

Nicole Bibbins Sedaca
Freedom House

Bryan Sims
Humanity United

Anthony Smith
Westminster Foundation for Democracy

Barbara Smith
The Carter Center

Daniel Twining
(Task force co-chair)
International Republican Institute (IRI)

Damon Wilson
National Endowment for Democracy (NED)

Jianli Yang
Citizen Power Initiatives for China

Foreword

Apowerful autocratic wave is sweeping the globe. Over the last 17 years, no country remains untouched. Moving slowly in its first decade, and now with brazen haste, autocrats clamp down on their civil societies, coordinate strategies with each other, propagate authoritarian governance abroad, and engage in increasingly sharp attacks against democracies.

This represents an urgent national and international security threat. Any viable strategy to respond will require action on multiple fronts, including strengthening democratic resilience, exerting top-down and bottom-up pressure on autocratic regimes, and fostering coordination by a range of actors.

Within such a strategy, certain options hold great potential, and this Playbook expands on one of them. It focuses on how democracies can better support and enable nonviolent civil resistance movements fighting for rights, freedom, and justice—as well as impose costs on their autocratic adversaries. In doing so, it builds on an established body of research about the power of these movements, their vital role in advancing democracy and reversing authoritarianism, and best practices in working with them.

The authors concurrently recognize that engaging with movements can be complex. Civil resistance movements emerge and are driven by indigenous energy, and efforts to support them are not without risks. However, the Playbook offers guidance that can mitigate concerns, laying out a wide range of options for consideration, alongside principles and a framework to inform their use.

While we may not subscribe to every recommendation or conclusion contained herein, we believe this Playbook advances a critical line of inquiry. Policymakers in democracies should seriously reckon with its implications for how we meet the authoritarian threat and catalyze democratic resurgence.

Derek Mitchell
President,
National Democratic Institute (NDI)

Daniel Twining
President,
International Republican Institute (IRI)

Lisbeth Pilegaard
Member of the Board and Chair of the Executive Committee,
European Endowment for Democracy (EED);

Executive Director,
Danish Institute for Parties and Democracy (DIPD)

Damon Wilson
President and CEO,
National Endowment for Democracy (NED)

Introduction

"In retrospect, all revolutions seem inevitable. Beforehand, all revolutions seem impossible."

—Ambassador Michael McFaul

The security of the United States, democratic allies, and humanity's future depends significantly on the state of democracy worldwide.

Yet over the past seventeen years, authoritarianism has risen globally, while democracy shows alarming decline. Dictatorial regimes in China, Russia, Iran, Venezuela and many other countries have become more repressive. Meanwhile, democracies in all parts of the world have backslid, with some regressing completely into authoritarianism.

This playbook focuses on a key factor that can help reverse both of these trends. Popular civil resistance movements—using tactics such as strikes, boycotts, protests, and many other tactics of noncooperation—are historically one of the most powerful drivers of democracy worldwide.[1] They can play a central role in transforming authoritarian regimes and countering democratic backsliding. We offer recommendations for how the United States and democratic allies can adeptly support and enable these movements.

The stakes in this contest over global governance could not be higher. A more authoritarian world is a world dangerous for democracies. As autocrats support each other, abuse their own populations, and undermine democratic states, they also perpetrate and create conditions for violent conflict, atrocities, humanitarian crises, the growth of violent nonstate actors, subversion of multilateral institutions, and transnational corruption. These produce massive human suffering, and further exacerbate internal weaknesses of democratic governments, thereby creating a positive feedback loop that contributes greatly to the present-day autocratic wave.

Yet this threat can be countered. Three previous global democratic waves have emerged from democratic troughs. Developing a strategy to catalyze a fourth wave begins with a clear-eyed look at the challenges we currently face. Externally, democracies confront an increasingly existential conflict waged against them, with authoritarian governments using democratic openness to enable them to spread corruption, undermine government institutions, influence economic decision-making, and manipulate the information environment. Simultaneously, many democracies are experiencing legitimacy crises due to long-standing failure to deliver adequately for their constituents. This core weakness has made them more vulnerable to populism, polarization, disruptive information technologies, external authoritarian attacks, and internal demagogues who now use a well-trod path to weaken democratic governance from the inside out. Past denial about the potency of these threats enabled them to grow. Turning the tide now requires urgency, clear vision, strategy, collective action, discipline, and innovative tactics. Democracies must unify, strengthen their alliances, and go on offense because the future depends on it.

Any strategy to counter authoritarianism will entail action on multiple fronts. By articulating in this playbook how to better support and create an enabling environment for pro-democracy civil resistance movements, we focus on one of the greatest foreign policy opportunities available today—engaging the power potential of populations worldwide who want to protect and advance human rights and democratic rule. Our allies are found not only in fellow governments and registered civil society organizations, but also among billions of people who live daily under either weakening democracies or the abuse of dictatorship.

How This Playbook Is Organized

Bottom-up pressure by movements, complemented by sustained and coordinated action among democracies to support these movements and constrain autocratic regimes, can lead to democratic resurgence. To help make a fourth democratic wave a reality, this playbook outlines three pillars of an actionable, evidence-based plan, as well as policy recommendations for each. It proceeds as follows:

PART I: FOUNDATIONS

1. Civil Resistance Movements and Democratization

The dynamics of civil resistance movements are a basis for our approach. A groundbreaking body of research finds the powerful role that these movements play in driving democratic transitions against authoritarian rulers. An emerging body of research also finds their importance in strengthening democratic resilience against backsliding.

2. Democratic Waves and Analysis of Contemporary Trends

Democracy historically advances and retreats in waves that can span the globe. Following a vast expansion of freedom during the third democratic wave (1974-2006), the world has now entered a prolonged period of autocratization.[2] We highlight lessons from past waves, apply them to current global trends, and address implications for strategy moving forward.

PART II: A THREE-PILLAR STRATEGY TO FOSTER A FOURTH DEMOCRATIC WAVE

3. Pillar I: Broadening Options to Enable and Support Civil Resistance Movements

Strengthening support for movements holds great promise, but also requires willingness to make needed changes and new investments.

First, democracy support must be recognized as a key national interest, weighted accordingly in policy decisions, and influence a wide range of government activities. Concurrent with this, the definition of democracy itself must be more tightly bound to the presence of human rights. Such a shift in US foreign policy, backed up with action, will strengthen an enabling environment for movements.

Second, investment in new options, capacities, and modalities must be made to support pro-democracy civil resistance movements. To this end, we identify

a wide range of specific ways to engage with these movements, in different stages of movement growth, in different contexts, and by different actors (both governmental and nongovernmental).

4. Pillar II: Developing a New Normative Framework— the Right of Assistance

Collective actions by democratic governments, willing multilateral institutions, and international nongovernmental organizations (including advocacy and philanthropy) are key to reversing the authoritarian tide. Developing a shared framework—which we call the "right to assistance" (R2A)—can enable greater international participation and collaboration in such efforts.

Populations and civil society organizations in all countries have the right to request and receive certain forms of assistance, and external actors have the right to respond accordingly. Grounded in this recognition, R2A would (re)legitimize a range of forms of external support to nonviolent pro-democracy movements, foster expedient coordination among governments, and provide guidance to evaluate which movements may receive support, what forms of support are permissible, and related questions.

5. Pillar III: Strengthening Democratic Solidarity to Pressure and Constrain Repressive Regimes

A third pillar of strategy involves building solidarity and capacity among democracies to leverage behavior change in authoritarian regimes, increase the costs of their repression, and foment divisions among those regimes' supporters. To this end, we identify actions for coordinated pressure by leading democracies, provide a movement-centered context for their consideration and use, and advance additional options for implementation through existing entities such as the Group of Seven (G7), or possible new democratic coalitions.

PART III: WEIGHING RISKS AND OPPORTUNITIES

6. Addressing Questions About Implementation

The arguments and some of the recommendations in this playbook advocate for a reconsideration—or scaling up—of certain policies and activities related to supporting pro-democracy movements. We conclude by addressing several concerns that may be raised in discussions about this course of action.

Executive Summary

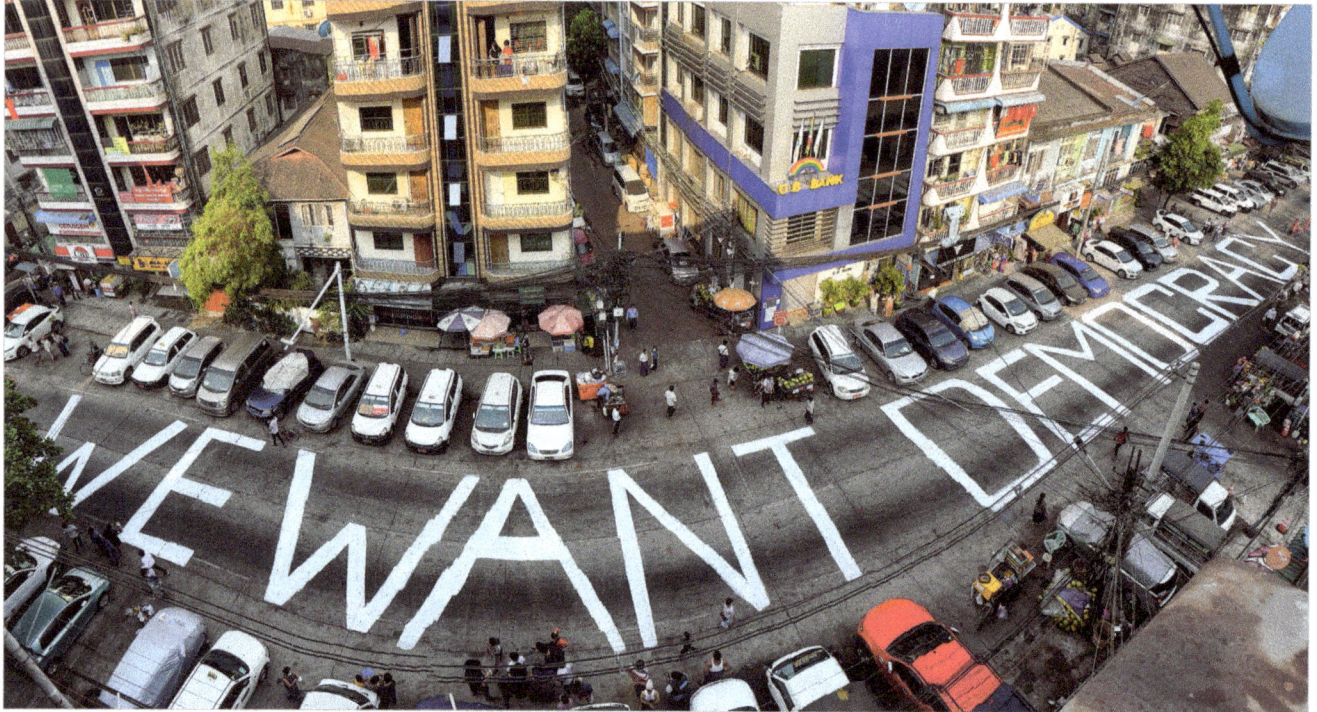

A slogan is written on a street as a protest after the coup in Yangon, Myanmar February 21, 2021. Picture taken with iPhone panoramic mode. REUTERS/Stringer

This playbook is based on the following premises:

- The global rise of authoritarianism is a national and international security threat. As autocrats support each other, abuse their own populations, and undermine democratic states, they are creating a world fundamentally hostile to democracy. Therefore, countering authoritarianism and supporting democracy are key national interests, and demand powerful strategies, innovative tactics, and long-term resolve.

- Established research finds that civil resistance movements are one of the most powerful drivers of democratic change over the last century. This means that bottom-up pressure is fundamental to countering authoritarianism and supporting democracy, and top-down efforts to advance these goals should seek greater alignment with movements.

- Civil resistance movements are driven by thousands or millions of people choosing to exercise their human rights and demand political change. They have the most at stake in the fight for human rights and democracy in their countries, and when they choose to rise up, democratic external actors must be prepared to draw on greater capacities and coordination to support them.

- Authoritarian regimes deeply fear civil resistance movements, and have, over the past two decades, put sustained effort into countering them, by harnessing new technologies and coordinating among themselves. Accordingly, movement success rates have declined significantly since 2010.

- External support for movements, if appropriately tailored, can improve their success rates. Movement support can be complex, but research and experience offer insights and best practices for assistance that can apply at different stages of movement growth.

- Common concerns about movement support include the risk of inadvertently harming movements, or contributing to political instability. These risks are navigable, and at times, inaction can contribute significantly to them. Averting potential harm to movements involves adoption of principles that ground support in listening and responding to the expressed needs of grassroots actors. Mitigating risks of instability involve incentivizing and supporting the use of nonviolent strategies, so that when populations choose to rise up, their movements are more likely to produce stable and democratic outcomes.

- External support can be enhanced and will be seen as more legitimate if it is grounded in a broadly accepted norm of a "right to assistance"—that is, people have a right to request and receive assistance when they are engaged in efforts to foster democracy and protect human rights. Democracies should take steps to articulate and advance such a norm.

- Complementing bottom-up pressure of movements, democracies have a range of coercive pressures that they can exercise on autocratic regimes to significantly deter their repression and enhance the political space for these movements to succeed. Such democratic efforts will be stronger if they are taken multilaterally. In addition, a more systematic, tiered approach—in which external responses to autocratic regimes are linked directly to their level of repressive activity against movements—is likely to have a stronger deterrent effect on these regimes.

Building from these premises, we outline three pillars of an actionable, evidence-based plan:

I.   Broadening options to enable and support civil resistance movements.

II. Developing a new normative framework: the right to assistance (R2A).

III. Strengthening democratic solidarity to pressure and constrain repressive regimes.

Pillar I: Broadening Options to Enable and Support Civil Resistance Movements

The backbone of movement support is a democracy-centered foreign policy. Well-organized civil resistance movements use every bit of political space available to them. International support for freedoms of expression, assembly, association, press, and other human rights—as well as substantial pressure on regimes that violate these freedoms—creates an enabling environment for movements. In turn, on their own initiative, these movements can then more effectively push for changes that enable a democracy-centered foreign policy to succeed.

To achieve this, countering authoritarianism and protecting and supporting democracy must become recognized as key national interests—fully weighed in policy decisions—and influence a wide range of government activities. The definition of democracy itself must also become more tightly bound to the presence of human rights.

A second aspect of government support relates to specific forms of engagement with movements. The very qualities that make movements resilient and powerful can also make them challenging to assist. Movements tend to be somewhat fluid, depend on widespread voluntary participation, can operate in highly repressive environments, and have varying degrees of structure or organization. There is no simple formula for movement assistance, but past experience and research establish several baselines for how to approach this task.

The first baseline is that **external support should be seen as an extension of—rather than a substitute for—a movement developing the necessary domestic participation, organization, attributes, and strategy to win on the ground.**

Second, **external actors should actively solicit movement requests for assistance, support local ownership and empowerment, and be flexible as local partners determine how best to apply the support received.**

Third, **the impact of movement support can be strengthened when external actors coordinate.**

Within these parameters, external support strategies can be developed based on understanding the challenges, opportunities, and needs that movements experience over five phases of development that we outline below:

1. Early organizing.

2. Peak mobilization.

3. Protracted struggle.

4. Transition.

5. Post-transition.

In particular, the "early organizing" and "peak mobilization" phases are fundamental to shaping a movement's trajectory and subsequent prospects for success.

Phase 1: Early Organizing

During this beginning but critical phase, activists aim to form a movement, and appropriate external assistance can make a major impact with relatively small investment. Yet most external actors fail to recognize early organizing as an opportunity for support, and instead tend to pay attention to movements only at later phases (i.e., once the movement encounters public repression).

Challenges and opportunities faced by movements in the early organizing phase include convening and training to develop a core group of leaders; strategic assessment and planning for all remaining phases of the movement (through even the post-transition phase); increasing public awareness about the prospect of civil resistance; building unity among supporters for shared goals and a positive vision for the movement; and relationship and trust building with representatives of key groups that will enable the movement to increase mobilization when it is ready.

Key support activities for external actors during this phase include:

- Investing in educational infrastructure related to civil resistance.

- Supporting strategic planning.

- Facilitating convenings and dialogue to foster unity and lay the groundwork for subsequent widespread movement participation.

- Helping activists to navigate choices around technology use.

- Providing modest funding, under certain conditions, to support these and related activities.

Phase 2: Peak Mobilization

In this phase, movements trigger public confrontation with their opponents, and seek to make their actual mobilization match the mobilization potential that they developed in the early organizing phase. As the movement's visibility rises, it starts to face targeted repression.

Challenges and opportunities faced by movements in the peak mobilization phase involve making repression backfire, maintaining nonviolent discipline in the face of regime provocations, and inducing defections from a regime's pillars of support.

Key support activities for external actors during this phase include:

- Taking actions to deter regime repression, raise its cost, and mitigate its impacts.

- Offering ongoing strategy development support.

- Helping movements to maintain nonviolent discipline.

- Building international coalitions to pressure the regime.

- Offering critical information to movements about ongoing developments.

- Fostering communications with potential regime defectors.

Phase 3: Protracted Struggle

Protracted struggle occurs when peak mobilization has passed (as a result of repression or a movement's temporary exhaustion), but both the regime and the movement persist and continue to contend. While not all movements go through this phase (sometimes a single peak mobilization can achieve a movement's goals), many movements experience protracted struggle, which can last for years and may be punctuated by additional periods of peak mobilization.

During this time, disappointment can set in. Mobilizing involves elevating hopes, and long pent-up emotions can suddenly manifest with urgency. However, the average civil resistance movement seeking maximalist goals (either a political transition, self-determination, or ending a foreign occupation) lasts for three years, and it is important for movements to identify metrics to help them track their progress and focus their efforts during this time.[3]

Challenges and opportunities in the protracted struggle phase involve sustaining movement engagement over longer periods of time, continuing to build movement strength (i.e., ongoing training efforts and coalition building) and offensive capacities against the regime, continuing to refine strategic and future transition planning, and building structures within movements that can help it endure.

Key support activities for external actors in this phase include:

- Drawing from repertoires used in both the early organizing phase (i.e., strategic planning support to help a movement regroup) as well as the peak mobilization phase (i.e., building international pressure on the regime, raising the cost of repression, mitigating repression's impact, and fostering defections).

- Using a period of protracted struggle to increase coordination with other external actors.

- Agreeing to offer help, if activists request it, to mediate directly between the movement and the regime.

Phase 4: Transition

The transition phase occurs when there is a formalized process to accommodate movement demands. In some cases, this takes place during a short period of negotiation, lasting days or weeks. In others, such as an election, there are aspects of negotiation (i.e., throughout a political campaign, assembling a winning coalition, and making personnel appointments upon victory), and there may also be an interregnum between the election and a candidate assuming office. However, not all movements experience a transition phase, since some transition mechanisms—i.e., a resignation of a leader or a coup d'état—happen suddenly with little formal process or warning.

Challenges and opportunities in the transition phase include maintaining movement mobilization, leverage and unity, and negotiating durable agreements that can form the foundation of a future democratic status quo.

Key support activities for external actors can involve:

- Encouraging movements to seek negotiated or electoral transitions, when possible.

- Supporting negotiations by setting up a brain trust, sometimes with help from diaspora populations, to provide ideas and contextual and specialized knowledge relevant to democratic political transitions (i.e., legal matters and transitional justice processes).

- Pledging future economic support and security, which can assure fence-sitters that any transition will be orderly, with prospects of economic growth and stability.

- Discouraging coups and warning of their consequences.

Phase 5: Post-transition

The post-transition phase occurs when the movement has achieved its primary goal, and now must consolidate and protect its gains. During this phase, a movement's unity risks fragmenting, demobilization becomes more likely, and a movement's opponents often start quietly to plot a comeback.

Challenges and opportunities involve holding a new government to its commitments, maintaining popular pressure on institutions to uphold the rule of law, advocating for accountability for past perpetrators of abuse, remaining vigilant about attempts at an authoritarian comeback, and ensuring that any future civil resistance serves to strengthen democracy and not undermine it.

Key support activities for external actors in this phase include:

- Engaging in traditional forms of democracy assistance and institution building.

- Supporting economic growth and state security, as needed.

- Advocating the adoption of laws and practices that protect human rights and civic space.

- Being ready to play a watchdog role when a new government is confronted by its own mobilized nonviolent citizenry.

Pillar II: Developing a New Normative Framework—the Right to Assistance (R2A)

Collective actions by democratic governments, willing multilateral institutions, and international nongovernmental organizations are all important in movement support efforts. Developing a shared normative framework—a broadly recognized right to assistance (R2A)—could go a long way toward legitimizing support for nonviolent civil resistance movements and enabling greater international participation and collaboration in such efforts.

The concept behind R2A is straightforward: **regardless of where they live, people have the right to request and receive assistance in order to protect and advance fundamental human rights**.

Advancing this normative framework would directly challenge autocratic governments that have asserted, with increasing success over the past two decades, their own de facto norm of "hyper-sovereignty." Based on this norm, they grant themselves carte blanche to engage in domestic repression, curtail international efforts to support democracy, and brazenly block accountability for themselves and their allies in the United Nations and other fora. Meanwhile, they also betray their own arguments by aggressively attacking and undermining democratic states.

The right to assistance would be grounded in international law, but would not depend on the UN for formal invocation. Rather, it would be developed and embraced by a coalition of democracies (such as the Group of Seven [G7], a group of democracies similar to the Democracies 10 [D-10], or a broader democratic alliance), and its initial formulation would be based on three premises.

The right to assistance is an extension of existing, internationally recognized human rights.

Numerous relevant international and regional treaties, UN General Assembly resolutions, and statements and practices of other international institutions (such as the Human Rights Committee and other treaty-established entities) provide support for a right to assistance. In particular, the right to freedom of association enables both formal and informal groups to request, receive, and use a wide variety of resources.

Therefore, to advance R2A, a group of democracies first needs to come to agreement about, and potentially codify, clear minimum standards about how they respect their populations' right to assistance, and then call on other states, many of whom are signatories to international human rights treaties, to equally respect their population's human rights by meeting these standards.

Acts of civil resistance are protected under international human rights law.

The introduction of a right to assistance will be met by regimes claiming that their civil society restrictions are based on "sound" national security grounds. Authoritarians label civil resistance as foreign-backed regime change in an attempt to justify their crackdowns and marginalize human rights concerns. They characterize popular nonviolent movements demanding democracy as a foreign act of war, a criminal conspiracy, or a terrorist threat.

Unsurprisingly, these conspiratorial claims are not grounded in fact. Civil resistance movements are driven by widespread, voluntary mobilization by people in a society seeking to redress their grievances and/or achieve their aspirations. Moreover, many acts of civil resistance involve the exercise of legally protected human rights. Mass demonstrations, boycotts, labor strikes, and numerous other nonviolent actions enact human rights enshrined in numerous treaties.

A government's sovereignty and the norm of nonintervention are not absolute.

A government's sovereignty ultimately derives from the population it governs. Thus a head of state can only legitimately claim sovereignty when the country's population has regular opportunities to exercise their rights of self-determination to vest their sovereignty (temporarily, until the next election or other democratic process) in that head of state.

Furthermore, claims of government sovereignty also come with responsibility. Sovereignty does not give a government free reign to suspend human rights—rather, it entails a responsibility to uphold and protect them.

Therefore, when an autocrat denies their population's right to self-determination, and further violates the population's human rights when they rise up to demand redress, the autocrat's claim to sovereignty becomes porous. This opens the possibility of escalating forms of intervention to protect and restore the rights of the population.

Ultimately, R2A will only be as strong as the unity of those who stand behind it, and their willingness to take action accordingly.

Pillar III. Strengthening Democratic Solidarity to Pressure and Constrain Repressive Regimes

As democratic states develop better methods to enable and support movements, they must also increase their solidarity and develop improved strategies to go on offense. These activities are interrelated because imposing costs on autocrats means autocrats will respond in kind. Greater unity and strength among democracies enable greater democratic offense.

Three aspects of this are outlined below.

Building Democratic Solidarity and Capacities to Constrain Authoritarians

Democracies stand a better chance of pressuring autocrats if they can align policies and actions. The G7 provides an existing platform for influential democracies to act, and its members constitute over fifty percent of global gross domestic product. However, the G7 is limited to major transatlantic democracies plus Japan, and in the face of common threats, there are opportunities to form wider coalitions.

One option is the establishment of an informal working group that consists of leading democracies. Alternatively, the United States and its allies could establish a new standing body, such as D-10 or a broader coalition of democracies, with a mandate to develop strategy and coordinate execution of joint efforts to support democracy and counter authoritarian efforts. The informal working group, or new standing body, would engage perspectives from every major region to identify threats and develop solutions to address them.

Whatever its form, an alliance of influential democracies could impose costs on autocratic regimes, incentivize their behavior change, and develop mechanisms to provide assistance to targeted democracies. As a core function, it could use its economic influence to defend against external attacks.

The alliance could also help invigorate support for pro-democracy movements around the world by advancing the norm of a right to assistance, and adopt coordinated approaches and tools to support civil resistance move-

ments through all phases of development. More broadly, it could orchestrate impactful public engagement efforts to highlight the dangers of authoritarianism, and the instrumental value and tangible benefits of democracy, aimed at influencing audiences around the world.

Raising the Cost of Autocratic Repression and Subversion

A democratic alliance, or any grouping of democracies, can take coordinated actions to constrain and impose costs on authoritarian regimes, including the following actions.

HEIGHTENING VISIBILITY OF REGIME AND MOVEMENT ACTIONS

External actors can monitor developments, draw attention to regime abuses, and condemn them through multiple channels. They also can elevate voices from a movement and highlight examples of courageous and strategic civil resistance. For example, visiting dignitaries can assign the same priority to meetings with civil society groups as they do with foreign government officials. Diplomats may engage in coordinated actions with their counterparts from other democratic states to show collective presence and support for human rights and democracy. They can further attend activist trials and observe public movement activities, thereby serving as monitors and an indirect protective presence. Governments also can provide greater support to independent media.

WITHDRAWING SUPPORT

Research finds that withdrawal of state support from autocrats can be "pivotal" to the success of civil resistance movements.[4] This is logical, since it signals an autocrat's declining international support, challenges the legitimacy of the regime's recent actions, denies it practical material or other assistance, and can cause people within a regime's domestic pillars of support to question the regime's sustainability. Examples of this include France's withdrawal of support for the Ben Ali government in Tunisia, and the United States' ultimate withdrawals of support from the Mubarak regime in Egypt, the Pinochet regime in Chile, and the Marcos regime in the Philippines.

COORDINATING SANCTIONS

A democratic alliance could coordinate targeted sanctions on individuals and entities that perpetrate human rights abuse and corruption. These sanctions aim to isolate their targets from resources and deprive them of the benefits of living in a globalized world, which means that the more countries that implement them, the more powerful they are.

The most effective sanctions often start with research, civil society input, and intelligence assessments to identify the individuals and entities that should be targeted. In addition, once sanctions are imposed, the target seeks to evade them and find alternative means of gaining resources, and this also requires regular and ongoing efforts to map evolving illicit relationships and expand sanctions to the target's environment.

Coordination on the above efforts is already happening multilaterally, but its scope and scale should be significantly expanded.

This calls for a more systematic approach, built on greater intelligence and research capacities, as well as clearer standards and consistency of application. A democratic alliance could operate as a de facto global sanctions coordinating body. In addition, criteria for sanctions could be expanded. Already human rights abuse and corruption are considered justifiable grounds for sanctions—perhaps undermining democracy may be included as additional grounds in the future.

JUDICIAL ACCOUNTABILITY

In addition to heightened monitoring and implementation of sanctions, democracies can also establish formal investigatory capacities to build dossiers on perpetrators, for referral to relevant judicial bodies. When regime perpetrators know that the cloak of anonymity will be lifted—that they will likely be named, personally sanctioned, and referred for criminal prosecution—it could have a deterrent effect.

The International Criminal Court, the establishment of ad hoc international tribunals, and reliance on national courts (under the theory of universal jurisdiction) are all potential options.

If a mechanism can be established in a particular case, a further challenge is for democracies to ensure that those engaged in violent repression are taken into custody and brought to justice. Democracies would need to establish a systematic approach for doing so. Notably, this effort could also play into an escalatory framework as discussed subsequently—whereby at certain thresholds of repression, greater resources would be allocated to automatically triggered investigations.

LEVERAGING CAPACITY FOR DEMOCRATIC MILITARY PERSUASION

A further way to undermine authoritarianism is through military influence. Democratic militaries have extensive contacts with other militaries worldwide—through exchange and educational programs, delegations, joint exercises, and international conferences. These points of contact present opportunities, if democracies prepare their officers and soldiers accordingly.

There are substantial institutional and individual benefits to military service under a democratic government instead of an authoritarian one. Understanding these benefits, as well as the often-unspoken sources of dissatisfaction of serving under authoritarian rule, can help democratic service members engage more effectively in advancing democratic attitudes in their personal and professional interactions with foreign counterparts.

In addition, when authoritarians crack down on movements, military and defense officials in democratic governments should develop strategies to leverage their extensive points of formal and informal contact to influence the decisions of their security forces. With preparation, such efforts by democracies can become proactive, systematic, and more coordinated among democracies internationally, and potentially tip the balance at key moments for pro-democracy movements.

DISRUPTING MALIGN INFLUENCE OPERATIONS

Democracies should also increase their efforts to inhibit major propagators of authoritarianism, such as the Chinese and Russian governments, by disrupting their foreign influence operations. A growing body of work identifies various ways that authoritarians exert influence in other countries' politics as well as proven strategies for preventing and countering this malign influence. Evidence points to three tools—or areas of support—available for limiting malign influence or at least mitigating its impact.

First, democracies can provide support to activists to uncover, understand, and raise public awareness about the strategies and tactics foreign authoritarians use in each country to prop up a regime and expand their own influence inside the country's borders, and the impact of these efforts on vulnerable democracies. A second form of support involves equipping local stakeholders with the tools and resources to expose foreign malign influence; hold complicit leaders accountable; as well as devise and advocate for locally appropriate policy solutions to bolster democratic resilience and counter authoritarian influence.

Finally, democracies can provide support to catalyze dialogue between stakeholders and policymakers on viable solutions to mitigate malign influence, and then hold officials accountable for implementing them.

Constraining Authoritarian Behavior: A Tiered Response to Repression

To further deter authoritarian repression, democracies may develop a tiered framework for imposing costs in response to escalating domestic (and at times international) repression of civil resistance movements.

The following table provides a starting point for further discussion.

Framework for Tiered Response		
Repression Level	Repression Characteristics (some or all listed characteristics may apply)	Potential Actions
Level One	• Disruption of movement operations. • Jailing movement members.	• Warning of reevaluation of security cooperation, trade, and aid relationships. • Strong diplomatic statements, including threats of personal (i.e. Magnitsky) sanctions against regime officials.
Level Two	• Sustained disruption of movement operations. • Broader jailing of movement members. • Credible reports of torture to movement members in jails. • Deaths of several movement members.	• Revaluation of security cooperation and restrictions on technology exports. • Pressure on other regimes to withdraw support, and restrict security cooperation. • Economic sanctions on regime members and enablers. • Consideration of broader economic sanctions.
Level Three	• Widespread jailing of movement members. • Widespread killing of movement members.	• Broaden and deepen sanctions. • Secondary pressures against allies of the perpetrating regimes. • Removal from SWIFT network.* • Cyberattacks to disrupt regime coercive apparatus. • Derecognition. • Arrest and jail regime authorities.

*SWIFT STANDS FOR SOCIETY FOR WORLDWIDE INTERBANK FINANCIAL TELECOMMUNICATION.

Policy Recommendations

Pillar I: Broadening Options to Enable and Support Civil Resistance Movements

Recommendation #1: Elevate democracy as a key national interest.

- **The US government should elevate supporting democracy to be a central factor in foreign policy decision-making.** The president should direct the national security agencies and the national security advisor to weigh implications for democracy in all major foreign policy decisions. In addition, the president should issue a National Security Strategy or directive for supporting democracy overseas. Such a directive would send a strong signal to US allies and authoritarian regimes that the United States is committed to supporting democracy overseas.

- **The European Union and other democratic governments should implement similar measures** to ensure that supporting democracy and combatting authoritarianism are reflected as key national interests.

Recommendation #2: Invest in new options and coordination to support and foster the capacities of pro-democracy civil resistance movements.

- **Departments and agencies within the US government should set up working groups to review options and establish improved processes for supporting movements, and a US government-wide working group should be established to help coordinate support.** Establishing this government-wide "home" from which movement support can be coordinated, as well as working groups within individual departments and agencies, will facilitate increased collaboration on roles and responsibilities (i.e., securing visas, offering funding, developing sanctions), and thus more effective support.

- **The US Congress should establish a fund to support innovative programs aimed at reversing authoritarianism and providing assistance to civil resistance movements.** A pillar of this fund should focus on building core infrastructure to support movements (i.e., educational and skill-building initiatives, efforts to promote unity among opposition groups), and resourcing cutting-edge programs to revitalize stalled—or cement gains of surging—democratic movements. Congress should mandate to the executive branch that innovation—and risk taking—are requirements. To win the conflict with authoritarians and their enablers, new resources will be essential.

- **With the White House leading, executive branch agencies that are the primary funders of democracy assistance**—the US Agency for International Development (USAID) and the Department of State—**need to be more forward leaning in providing support to civil resistance movements.** This will entail USAID and the Department of State eliciting and welcoming novel programmatic approaches, many not tried before, for supporting movements, as well as understanding—and accepting—that there will be some failure. Funding should provide flexibility to the implementer to pivot targets and spending, based on movement needs, and allow multiyear awards, which will allow partners and movements to conduct medium- to long-term planning.

- **Democratic governments should increase the quantity and amount of multiyear funding to increase movement training and skill building,** providing such funds to nongovernmental organizations. Allies should prioritize support for rapid small grants for equipment, transport, convening space, and other short-term movement needs.

- **Democratic governments should support establishment of international strike funds,** i.e., through grants to international nongovernmental organizations, and increase resources available for urgent/emergency assistance to activists under threat, through new or existing capabilities like the lifeline assistance fund or other USAID rapid response capacities.

- **Democratic governments should use their convening power** to bring together international nongovernmental organizations (advocacy and philanthropy), CSOs, diaspora groups, and movement activists (if possible, given the local context and security situation) during nascent movement stages to discuss coordination of external support.

2019 Hong Kong anti-extradition law protest on June 16, captured by Studio Incendo from Flickr.

- **Democratic governments should support activists gathering and engaging in dialogue**, crafting a common vision for the future of their country, and planning and developing unity on elements of democratic transition plans. Brain trusts may also be developed to advise on transition processes (i.e., legislative or constitutional changes, transitional justice processes) or other phases of a movement's growth.

- **Democratic governments should expand the quantity of multiyear funding available to support the growth of educational infrastructure** for activists internationally through international nongovernmental organizations. More is needed to resource new research and the development of new educational resources in civil resistance, which can be made freely available, in English and other languages. Useful research can be academic or applied, and focus on topics that activists or external actors have predefined as being relevant to their work. New educational resources would take generic civil resistance insights and localize them to particular regions, focusing on particular regional issues (i.e., countering corruption), drawing on relevant regional

examples, and being available in relevant regional languages.

- **Democratic governments should dedicate resources to support initiatives aimed at advancing an enabling legal environment for human rights movements**. Such initiatives should include: a) advocacy to reform laws that are used to chill and punish nonviolent collective action, and advocacy to promote enabling legislation; b) tools and activities to help activists and movements navigate restrictive legal environments; and c) emergency legal and financial assistance and other vital protection for movement members who are targeted.

Recommendation #3: Augment and reposition diplomatic services to enhance movement support.

- **Democratic governments should organize their embassies to enhance outreach to movements.** Embassies in key countries should dedicate at least one political officer to proactively broaden their contacts to engage with movement actors as well as regularly monitor and analyze movement developments. This will involve an expansive concept of civil society, and include reaching out to groups and associations that may be small, community-based, unregistered, and/or outside of major cities. This political officer should work to develop options for movement support and communicate with allied embassies to coordinate support. Governments can dedicate additional communications staff in embassies in key countries when movement activity is anticipated or ongoing.

- **Democratic governments should provide increased diplomatic training on civil resistance movements and transitions**. The US Foreign Service Institute, USAID University, and similar training institutes in other democracies, should add modules on civil resistance and democratic transitions (i.e., how civil resistance works, principles of external support) and make these courses a mandatory part of foreign service officer training. Professional development seminars should also be proactively held in missions abroad. The US State Department and other foreign ministries should provide greater professional incentives (career advancement, promotions, awards, and public recognition) for foreign service officers to specialize in human rights work and directly engage with civil society.

Recommendation #4: Support independent media internationally and locally.

- **Democratic governments should significantly increase funding and technical assistance to create infrastructures of support for independent media.** Such support may aim to increase independent international news coverage, local news outlets, and movement-based media outlets. The presence of these forms of media are associated with positive impacts for civil resistance movements. Funding and technical assistance could help with start-up costs, the development of effective business models, internal governance and accountability structures, investigative journalism, journalist training and education, the establishment of professional associations, and efforts to protect journalists and media outlets under threat.

- **Democratic governments should coordinate to vigorously push back against attempts to intimidate, silence, or restrict free press.** Attacks on free press should be seen as a leading indicator of democratic backsliding, and trigger swift multilateral responses.

Pillar II: Developing a New Normative Framework—the Right to Assistance (R2A)

Recommendation #5: Establish a multilateral task force to develop R2A.

- **Democratic governments should establish a multilateral task force to assess the feasibility of advancing an internationally recognized right to assistance**, potentially under the auspices of the G7 or another entity comprised of leading democracies.

- **Democratic governments should launch formal multi-stakeholder dialogues on the potential design, adoption, and implementation of a right to assistance**, involving and seeking input and comment from governments, international nongovernmental organizations (advocacy and philanthropy), CSOs, diaspora groups, and activists. The principals administering these dialogues should be adequately resourced so as to be able proactively reach out to groups, substantively interact with them, and seek their comments; and be able to allocate research funds when needed to support the development of international legal, strategic, or other aspects of designing, adopting, and implementing a right to assistance.

Recommendation #6: Renew commitment to key international human rights laws and norms.

- **Democratic governments should renew and expand their efforts to defend international human rights law and norms**, in particular those relating to the freedoms of association, assembly, and expression. Moreover, such governments must actively defend civil resistance, and support to it, as consistent with internationally recognized and protected human rights.

- **Democratic governments should increase their engagement with multilateral organizations that create and uphold international human rights norms** and provide mechanisms to raise the diplomatic and reputational costs when those norms are violated by authoritarian states.

Pillar III: Strengthening Democratic Solidarity to Pressure and Constrain Repressive Regimes

Recommendation #7: Establish a new entity of leading democracies.

- **Democratic governments should establish a new coordinating entity for advancing democracy.** A new coordinating mechanism, established through the G7 or a new coalition of democracies, could spearhead a campaign to empower democratic movements around the world. This should include moral, legal, and financial assistance to people who are on the ground working to advance democracy and under the threat of retribution by authoritarian regimes or their local proxies. The new entity would also act as an active repository of research and analysis to identify targets for sanctions, and to harmonize their implementation.

Recommendation #8: Establish a mechanism to hold accountable regime officials involved in the suppression of democracy.

- **Democratic governments should establish an internal mechanism to investigate and document unlawful or illegitimate actions taken by officials in authoritarian regimes that violently repress civil resistance movements.** Such a mechanism can be housed within the justice ministries or investigative bureaus of these governments.

- **Democracies should join together within a multilateral framework to hold accountable such officials.**

Recommendation #9: Assign defense agencies to take a more active role in democracy support.

- **Democratic governments should assign their respective departments or ministries of defense with taking a more active role in democracy support.** Defense officials and military officers from democracies should seek to influence their counterparts in autocratic countries to support democratic change and strengthening in their own countries. When authoritarians crack down on movements, military and defense officials in democratic governments should redouble such efforts.

Recommendation #10: Develop a systematic framework with escalating responses to deter violent repression.

- **The United States should establish a government-wide working group to develop a tiered framework of escalating responses to violent repression.** The United States should work with leading democracies to build a framework for collective action centered around enforcement of this tiered approach.

- **Other leading democracies should establish a similar mechanism**, and ensure that these efforts are coordinated.

Recommendation #11: Scale up funding to counter foreign malign influence.

- **The United States should scale up funding dedicated to countering foreign malign influence in third countries.** Funding should center on increasing the resilience of governments and civil society against attempts by authoritarian governments such as the People's Republic of China and the Russian government—the two most powerful actors opposed to democracy worldwide—to erode democracy and coopt elites.

PART 1

Foundations

1. Civil Resistance Movements and Democratization

Civil resistance is a way that ordinary people wield power without the threat or use of physical violence. It has played a leading role in numerous political transitions against authoritarian rule—such as the ousters of Ferdinand Marcos (Philippines, 1986), Augusto Pinochet (Chile, 1988), Soviet rulers in Eastern and Central Europe (1989-91), Slobodan Milošević (Serbia, 2000), Victor Yanukovich (Ukraine, 2014), Zine al-Abidine Ben Ali (Tunisia, 2011), Hosni Mubarak (Egypt, 2011), Blaise Compaoré (Burkina Faso, 2014), Abdelaziz Bouteflika (Algeria, 2019), and Omar al-Bashir (Sudan, 2019). Notably, autocrats in each of these (and many other) countries were widely assumed to be stable and firmly in control prior to their ousters.

Civil resistance also plays a critical role in building democratic strength. It has expanded democratic rights and freedoms in countries like the United States (i.e., the Civil Rights Movement, the labor movement, and women's suffrage movement), and countered corruption and backsliding in countries like North Macedonia (2014-16), Slovakia (2017), South Korea (2017), Armenia (2018), Ecuador (2015-17), and Sri Lanka (2022).

To varying degrees, people in these and other countries self-organized, fostered unity, strategized, and exerted powerful pressure through a range of nonviolent actions. Hundreds of civil resistance tactics exist, and the concept is defined by three kinds of acts:[5]

- **Acts of commission**, in which people deliberately engage in behaviors that are unexpected or forbidden. Examples include mass demonstrations, displaying symbols or messages, certain acts of civil disobedience, occupying buildings, and blockades.

- **Acts of omission** (sometimes referred to as "noncooperation"), in which people refuse to act in ways that are expected or government mandated. Examples of such acts include consumer boycotts, labor strikes, withdrawal of bank deposits, tax refusal, divestment, social boycotts, and election boycotts.

- **Combinations of acts of commission and omission**, including the establishment of alternative governance bodies (i.e., governments-in-exile, community dispute resolution bodies, local community councils), economic entities (i.e., alternative income-generating structures, strike funds, labor unions), educational institutions (i.e., home schools, underground publishing houses) and other structures (i.e., alternative media).

Understanding Nonviolent Power

Civil resistance works because rulers are vulnerable to disobedience. Authoritarians (or demagogues who seek to erode democracy) rely on large numbers of people to carry out direct orders, and also depend indirectly on vast numbers of people in society engaging in predictable economic, social, and political behaviors. Therefore, these rulers' sources of power can be severed—for example, laborers may go on strike and transportation workers may refuse to ship goods. Consumers can stop buying from targeted companies, banks can close, and students can boycott schools. Bureaucrats may quietly grind government to a halt, and security forces can deliberately work slowly and inefficiently.

Simultaneously, through the process of engaging in movement activities, people in society can develop new relationships, rebuild social fabric, develop shared identities, recast social polarization along new lines, learn new skills, redirect resources, and establish new formal and informal organizations. These qualities and effects often build democratic strength and resilience.

Thus, when movements engage in civil resistance in strategic and targeted ways, they can shift the balance of power in society—creating coercive leverage on corrupt and autocratically inclined rulers—and foster democratic development. There is a generalized six-stage process by which this happens.

The Difference between Protests and Civil Resistance Movements

Many people conflate the tactic of street protests with civil resistance. However, a protest demonstration is simply one of hundreds of tactics of civil resistance, and popular movements that defeat dictatorship tend to do so by sequencing diverse tactics—to generate social, economic, and political pressure—over time.

Civil resistance is also far more effective when it is employed by **movements**. Movements combine widespread voluntary participation with organization, and persist over time.

Movement leaders create structured campaigns to channel mobilization in accordance with a strategy to achieve clear goals. In contrast, protest demonstrations that are disconnected from movements are an example of mobilization without organization. As such, they are unlikely to threaten an autocrat's power, or produce long-term impacts, although sometimes movements can later emerge out of initially disorganized protests.

These distinctions are essential for strategy development. Efforts to foster a fourth democratic wave should center on approaches that enable and support the development of civil resistance movements and campaigns, rather than simply seeking to increase protest activity.

How Civil Resistance Movements Drive Democratic Change: A Six-stage Process

The process below describes a trajectory from initial mobilization of a civil resistance movement to a full political transition (i.e., the incumbent steps down from power). All six stages—which can happen over a span of weeks or years, depending on the case—are often required when a dictator is entrenched and willing to use escalating repressive means to try to remain in power.

In contrast, in cases of democratic backsliding, all six stages may not be required. If confidence remains that an elections system or formal accountability mechanism remains viable, civil resistance can preferably strengthen the use of those institutional channels, thereby constraining an autocratically inclined leader (as seen in stage four below, for example) until a scheduled election or other constitutional remedy can create an orderly transfer of power.[6]

However, there is no one-size-fits all strategy: each context and circumstance is different. It is not for outsiders to decide, but rather it is the actions of a ruler, and his/her willingness to order escalating repression and abuse, that determines how far a movement must escalate to counter them.

STAGE 1: CIVIL RESISTANCE IMPOSES COSTS

When people deliberately shift their behavior and obedience patterns, it raises the cost of maintaining an oppressive system. The greater the number of people that engage in noncooperation and disobedience (whether subtle or overt), and the more strategic those people are in their actions, the more resources and effort a government must expend to stabilize the status quo.

STAGE 2: CONCESSIONS AND REPRESSION FURTHER INCREASE POPULAR MOBILIZATION

In response to civil resistance, those in power may offer concessions, order repression, or pursue both strategies simultaneously to try to divide people, and/or make them passive and obedient.

However, concessions may encourage further resistance, because they can increase people's confidence that systemic change is possible. At the same time, repression can backfire by increasing outrage and nonviolent mobilization.

Therefore, both concessions and repression carry risks for a government. Both also place an additional cost on those individuals and groups trying to maintain the oppressive system.

STAGE 3: SPLITS EMERGE, PUBLIC SENTIMENT SHIFTS

Faced with sustained civil resistance, cracks that were previously latent begin to appear among a ruler's pillars of support.

This happens as some people realize that they will be expected to take increasing risks (i.e., confronting crowds of people with repression) and absorb greater costs (i.e., damage to reputation, lost profits) by remaining obedient to the ruler. For example, members of the business community may realize that ongoing acquiescence to an oppressive status quo has intolerable implications for their bottom line. Consequently, they may start to pressure the ruler to reach a settlement, or begin to support the opposition movement. At the same time, some street-level police and soldiers may begin to buckle at having to enforce orders that ultimately serve to protect their superiors, who are paid more and incur less day-to-day risk. Meanwhile, others who had previously supported an oppressive system (i.e., bureaucrats, members of state media and the judiciary, and government vendors) are forced to confront their role in it, perhaps by their own friends or family members. This cognitive dissonance, combined with social pressure to shift (including disapproval and loss of social status for continued obedience, but approval and respect for disobedience), can cause them to start to shift their loyalties and split off.

STAGE 4: DEFECTIONS AMONG FORMER SUPPORTERS

As previous supporters of an oppressive system shift their loyalties (which can manifest as becoming passive, neutral, critical of the status quo, or actively supportive of a civil resistance movement), those who continue to support the system begin to doubt its sustainability. This is so even among those who would prefer the repressive ruler remain in power. Once people start to think the ruler may lose, their own self-interest calculation changes, and they begin to wonder what will happen to them if they end up on "the wrong side of history." As a consequence, they consider other options to ensure their own security in case the ruler loses, and they begin hesitating in their own actions.

STAGE 5: COERCION AND TRANSITION

As doubts about a system's sustainability mount, these doubts become visible and reinforce the loyalty shifts of others, leading to defections among the system's critical supporters. Such defections can cascade quickly, and coerce power holders to accede to a movement's demands.[7] When a ruler gives repressive orders and they are no longer obeyed or are inadequate to restore the status quo, the ruler has no choice but to step down.

Whenever possible, to maximize democratic prospects thereafter, such a transfer should happen around an election (even if civil resistance is required to enforce the results) or through a structured negotiating process.[8] However, sudden and disorderly resignations by autocrats, coups, or even regime collapse are sometimes how such transitions take place, and while these dampen democratic outcomes, they do not erase the possibility of democratic gains.

STAGE 6: CONSOLIDATION

After an autocrat's rule ends, significant challenges remain. Other elements of the authoritarian system—such as corruption, inequitable concentration of power, and impunity—must be addressed. Existing government institutions, laws, and processes must also be modified, discarded, or wholly redeveloped based on democratic principles. Meanwhile, the economy and delivery of goods and services must continue, and previously suppressed societal tensions may create security challenges.

Post-transition civil resistance can help address some of these formidable circumstances. For example, nonviolent mobilization is a powerful way for ordinary citizens to ensure that any new political or economic bargains consider their needs and demands, especially when transitional decision-making processes offer them no formal seat at the table. Moreover, the social fabric, networks, capacities, skills, knowledge, structures, shared identities, resources, and confidence that were built through the course of civil resistance against an autocrat can be the foundation for a new active civil society that helps navigate societal conflicts and holds the new government and institutions to account.[9]

Movement Outcomes and Democratic Development

This aforementioned six-stage process outlines dynamics propelled by numerous civil resistance movements throughout history. But how frequently does this process happen—how often do movements win, and what are the outcomes?

An established body of research examines this question with regard to the use of civil resistance against authoritarian rule, and an emerging body of research offers insights on this question with regard to reversing democratic backsliding. We address both sets of findings below.

CIVIL RESISTANCE AGAINST AUTHORITARIAN RULE

Studies over the last decade identify a consistently strong relationship between civil resistance, political transitions, and democratic development. For example, between 1900 and 2019, civil resistance movements with maximalist goals (creating a political transition, expelling a foreign occupier, or achieving territorial independence) were found to achieve their goals 51 percent of the time. This is approximately twice the 26 percent success rate of violent insurgencies over this same time frame.[10]

Figure 1: Probability That a Country Will Be a Democracy Five Years After a Campaign Ends (1900-2006)

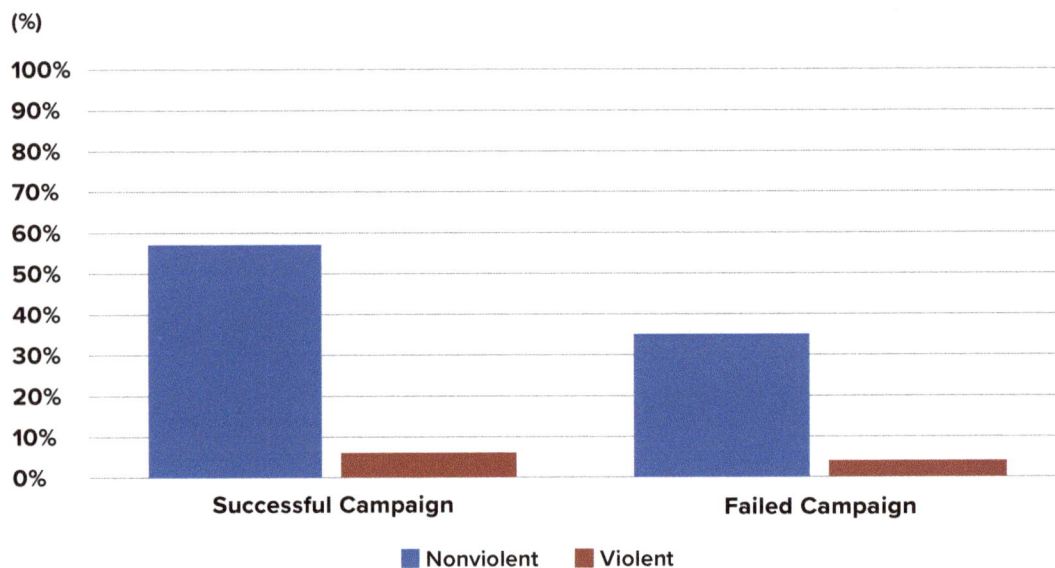

(%)

[Bar chart showing percentages from 0% to 100% in 10% increments]

Successful Campaign — Nonviolent approximately 57%, Violent approximately 6%

Failed Campaign — Nonviolent approximately 36%, Violent approximately 5%

■ Nonviolent   ■ Violent

SOURCE: Based on data from Erica Chenoweth and Maria J. Stephan, *Why Civil Resistance Works: The Strategic Logic of Nonviolent Conflict* (New York: Columbia University Press, 2011), 213-16.

Once a transition against an autocrat occurs, ensuing prospects for democracy and other stabilizing factors are also higher for civil resistance-led transitions. For example, between 1900 and 2006, 57 percent of maximalist civil resistance movements were found to result in democratic outcomes five years after achieving a political transition. In contrast, when a violent insurgency forced a political transition, it led to a democratic outcome only 6 percent of the time.[11]

Furthermore, even when a civil resistance movement *failed* to achieve its stated objectives, five years later there remained a 35 percent chance of a democratic outcome. This points to the fact that the process of movement organizing and engaging in nonviolent mobilization can plant the seeds for democratic growth, even when a movement does not immediately achieve its stated goals.[12]

Civil resistance-driven transitions against autocrats also significantly outperform elite-driven transitions in producing durable democratic gains. In one study evaluating sixty-seven cases between 1972 and 2004, elite-led transitions that did *not* involve popular nonviolent movements achieved a democratic outcome only 14 percent of the time.[13] In another study, political transitions from 1945 to 2015 that did *not* include significant civil resistance (such

as elite-driven transitions, but also violent insurgencies and coups) were found to lead to democracy only 29 percent of the time, versus 74 percent of the time for transitions that did.[14] Beyond this, civil resistance-driven transitions have been found to lead to greater economic growth than their top-down counterparts.[15]

Higher democratic stability also is a legacy of many nonviolent movements. The median lifespan of governments that result from civil resistance-driven transitions has been found to be forty-seven years, versus a median lifespan of nine years for transitions with no civil resistance movement (i.e., top-down transitions) and only five years for transitions driven by violent insurgencies.[16] Consistent with this, civil resistance-driven transitions are significantly more likely to lead to two or more successful electoral transfers of power (a sign that democracy has taken root), compared to transitions that do not involve civil resistance.[17]

Democratic quality also has been found to be relatively higher from civil resistance-driven transitions, particularly in the areas of freedom of expression and association.[18] Thus, as many members of the international democracy-promotion community focus on supporting democratic institutions and processes (i.e., elections), civil resistance movements are found to strengthen corresponding human rights that help sustain the democratic system. Moreover, the impact of movements extends beyond advances in rights: civil resistance-driven transitions are associated with rebounds in a country's life expectancy rate, when compared to transitions driven by violent insurgency.[19]

Faced with such compelling data and findings, some may assume that structural factors explain these discrepancies—arguing that civil resistance tends to occurs in "easier" contexts than violent insurgencies, or that it occurs in places that are more ripe for democracy. However, structuralist explanations have proven inadequate. As scholars Erica Chenoweth and Maria Stephan find: "The vast majority of nonviolent campaigns have emerged in authoritarian regimes...where even peaceful opposition against the government may have fatal consequences."[20] They have also succeeded against powerful governments, against a variety of regime types, in the face of violent repression, and in societies with varying levels of economic development and diverse ethnic characteristics.[21] Notably, they also work more quickly than violent insurgencies—with the average civil resistance movement lasting approximately three years, and the average violent insurgency lasting approximately nine years.[22]

CIVIL RESISTANCE AGAINST DEMOCRATIC BACKSLIDING

Compared to the use of civil resistance against authoritarian rule, civil resistance against democratic backsliding has received relatively less scholarly attention, and much of it has been qualitative.

Yet here, existing cases studies from multiple regions of the world, as well as recent research, also point to a similar democratizing influence. Broadly speaking, three kinds of domestic actors—institutions, opposition parties, and a wide array of civil society—have been identified as critical checks against backsliding.[23] Each has their function, and they can be most powerful when they exert simultaneous pressures on aspiring autocrats.[24] As backsliding continues over time, civil society in particular has often proven to be more durable than institutions, and hence plays a central role in countering many aspiring autocrats. Consistent with this, active civil society has been identified as a critical factor in reestablishing democracy once after a period of democratic breakdown.[25]

Numerous scholars also cite civil society, and particularly civic mobilization and civil resistance, as a safeguard of democracy. For example, in their sweeping study of polit-

Civil Resistance Movements and Political Parties

Civil resistance movements and political parties both seek to make political, economic, and social change, but there are distinctions between them. Movements tend to be more fluid and less structured than party organizations. They also tend to engage in outside-in strategies (i.e., nonviolent tactics to influence institutions and power relationships), as opposed to political parties that tend to rely on formal institutional strategies (i.e., elections, the legal system) of making change. However, much depends on context, and the degree of distinction or overlap between a movement's and party's membership, strategies, tactics, and policy goals will depend on societal conditions, and can also shift over time.

In overcoming encroaching or established authoritarian rule, both of these entities are often needed. For example, movements can be critical in driving up popular mobilization, voter turnout, raising issue awareness, influencing party platforms, shifting power relationships, fracturing ruling coalitions, and enforcing election results if there are attempts at subversion. Political parties, in turn, can be critically important partners for movements by adopting policy platforms and providing candidates that foster movement unity, negotiating, and helping to convert grassroots power into institutional changes. Political parties also play a pivotal role after political transitions in taking steps to consolidate democratic gains. At that point, some movement leaders may have also joined political parties, while other activists remain among the rest of civil society, continuing to advocate for change and accountability of the new government. Depending on the context, these activists may rely increasingly on organizational and institutional approaches to do so.

A demonstrator takes part in a protest against Nicaraguan President Daniel Ortega's government at the Metropolitan Cathedral in Managua, Nicaragua May 17, 2019. REUTERS/Oswaldo Rivas

ical transitions to dictatorship and democracy, scholars Stephan Haggard and Robert F. Kaufman conclude:

On balance...a weak and passive civil society and political opposition poses a far greater threat to the institutionalization of democratic politics than the occasional disruption it brings. Strong civil societies and vigorous political challenges to incumbents reduce the likelihood that the rules of the game will be restricted to "parchment documents." They raise the cost to the military of seeking to control the government, and increase incentives for them to pursue professional careers outside the political arena. A well-organized, robust, and dynamic civil society is also more likely to hold elected incumbents accountable to and reduce the chances for elite pacts made at the expense of the public. Viewed over the long run, the key to more stable democratic regimes may depend less on institutional design than on the societal organizations in which they are nested.[26]

Consistent with this conclusion, scholars Melis Laebens and Anna Lührmann examined how democratic backsliding can be effectively countered and conclude that:

For democratic erosion to be halted, civil society mobilization... against the government may be needed to trigger or support other accountability mechanisms. In all our cases [Benin, South Korea, and Ecuador], multiple accountability mechanisms involving pressure from the public and from political elites worked together to avert further democratic decline.[27]

Thus, from examples of popular mobilization countering corruption and power grabs in countries such as North Macedonia (2014-16), Slovakia (2017), South Korea (2017), Armenia (2018), Ecuador (2015-17), and Sri Lanka (2022), to research on the integral role of mobilized civil society in democratic development, it is clear that civil resistance is often a critical component of boosting democratic resilience and curtailing backsliding.

2. Democratic Waves and Analysis of Contemporary Trends

Scholars note that democratic practices and institutions have advanced rapidly at various periods in history, and identified three successive global waves of democracy over the last two centuries. They have also identified autocratic waves (sometimes also referred to as "reverse democratic waves") during which rising authoritarianism and democratic backsliding became prevalent trends. Merging insights on civil resistance with lessons from past waves, and applying these to current global circumstances, can offer guidance on how to foster a fourth democratic wave.

The First Waves

Political scientist Samuel Huntington identified the first democratic wave as occurring from 1828 to 1926, and it can be seen in the context of advancing support for democratic governance in lieu of monarchical rule.[28] Culminating in the collapse of European empires following World War I, emerging nations such as Lithuania, Estonia, Ukraine, Finland, Poland, Czechoslovakia, Yugoslavia, Romania, and others sought to legitimize themselves as sovereign nations and adopt democratic constitutions.[29] Countries like Argentina, Colombia, Uruguay, Japan, and New Zealand also moved toward democracy during this time period. By Huntington's count, the first wave brought into being about thirty governments that had "established at least minimal national democratic institutions" worldwide.[30] While many of these would be judged as nondemocracies by today's standards, they contained relatively more democratic institutions than other governments at the time.

However, this democratic wave came to an end by 1926 and began to recede. Commenting on the aftermath of World War I, Huntington writes: "The war that had been fought to make the world safe for democracy had instead unleashed movements of both the Right and the Left that were intent on destroying it."[31] Over the ensuing autocratic wave, attempts to accommodate extremists in government enabled them to grow stronger, and many of the nascent democratic institutions that emerged in Europe were overtaken by fascism and communism.[32] This authoritarian reversal lasted through World War II,

and left only twelve relatively democratic governments standing in its wake.[33]

The Second Waves

The second democratic wave began after the 1945 allied victory in World War II. The military defeat of fascist regimes cemented the ascent of democratic institutions and values, and led to campaigns of decolonization in numerous countries in Asia, Latin America, and Africa. People across the world rebelled against colonial rulers and declared independence, in part on the basis of democratic liberties that the allies had championed elsewhere.[34] At the high point of this wave, there were approximately fifty relatively democratic governments worldwide.[35]

This trend turned in 1962 and ushered in a twelve-year wave of autocratization, during which a number of electoral democracies in newly independent states backslid towards authoritarianism. Military coups also derailed dozens of democracies. At the low point of the second autocratic wave, the number of nominal democracies had decreased to approximately thirty.[36]

The Third Waves

The third democratic wave took place between 1974 and 2006, beginning with the Carnation revolution in Portugal, and followed by a host of democratic transitions in southern Europe, Latin America, Africa, and the Indo-Pacific region. With the collapse of communism and the fall of the Soviet Union in 1991, democratic diffusion across Eastern Europe and other parts of the world expanded further, particularly in countries that bordered existing democracies.

However, by the mid-1990s, this wave showed signs of weakening.[37] In the ensuing ten years, some states such as Serbia (2000), Georgia (2003), Ukraine (2004), and Nepal (2006) continued to democratize while other states began to autocratize. On balance, the rising democratic trend continued to 2006, by which point 58 percent of countries with populations over one million were classified as democratic.[38]

Defining and Labeling Democratic and Authoritarian Governments

There are numerous varieties of democratic, authoritarian, and hybrid regimes, and labeling countries as "democratic" or "nondemocratic" is not an exact science. The same government and society can contain some democratic and some authoritarian features, with different criteria leading to different classifications, and resulting in different counts of "democratic" or "nondemocratic" countries in the world at any given time.

While no single classification system is best for all purposes, we refer to two kinds of types of democracies ("electoral" and "liberal") and two types of autocracies ("electoral" and "closed"). These are defined by the V-Dem Institute as follows:*

Electoral democracy "meets sufficiently high levels of free and fair elections as well as universal suffrage, freedom of expression and association."

Liberal democracy includes criteria for "electoral democracy" as well as respect for "executive constraint by the legislature and high courts, rule of law and for individual rights."

Electoral autocracy contains "institutions emulating democracy but falling substantially below the threshold for democracy in terms of authenticity or quality."

Closed autocracy involves "an individual or group of people exercis[ing] power largely unconstrained by [the population]."

*SOURCE: VANESSA A. BOESE AND STAFFAN I. LINDBERG (EDS.). DEMOCRACY REPORT 2022: AUTOCRATIZATION CHANGING NATURE?, V-DEM INSTITUTE, UNIVERSITY OF GOTHENBURG, 2022, 13.

Thereafter, an autocratic wave prevailed and persists to this day. The last three decades of democratic advances have been reversed. As of 2022, liberal democracies have declined to their lowest levels in nearly thirty years, and now exist in approximately thirty-two nations, while electoral democracies exist in approximately fifty-eight. In contrast, electoral autocracy is now present in approximately fifty-six countries, and closed autocracies exist in approximately thirty-three countries. Collectively, the average level of democracy worldwide is estimated to have dropped to the same level it was in 1986.[39]

Insights from Past Waves

Insights from past and ongoing waves—particularly the third democratic wave and current seventeen-year autocratic wave—can inform future strategy development. To this end, we share several observations and lessons below, and discuss implications of each for fostering a fourth democratic wave.

1. **Civil resistance was a major factor in the third democratic wave.**

   Conventional wisdom tends to emphasize structural factors as driving the third democratic wave. For example, Huntington and others identified conditions such as global economic growth, the inability of authoritarian regimes to perform economically and sometimes militarily, the role of the Catholic church, and the foreign policies of the United States and Western Europe.[40]

   While these variables and top-down efforts had impacts, so too did bottom-up pressure in the form of civil resistance.[41] A study issued by Freedom House examined sixty-seven political transitions from nondemocratic governments between 1972 and 2004—which includes much of the third democratic wave—and concluded that fifty out of these sixty-seven transitions (75 percent) during this time period were driven in whole or in part by civil resistance, while only fourteen transitions (21 percent) were driven primarily by top-down, elite-led processes, and three occurred through foreign intervention. Furthermore, transitions driven by civil resistance were found to have a vastly greater probability of resulting in democratic outcomes (64 percent) than exclusively elite-led transitions (14 percent) or transitions that mixed opposition civil resistance and violence (20 percent).[42]

   Implications for a fourth democratic wave: Civil resistance will likely play a foundational role in the emergence and growth of a fourth democratic wave, and merits central consideration in foreign policy decisions on how to counter the authoritarian threat. Concurrently, top-down strategies to advance political changes are important but are not a substitute for the need for bottom-up civic pressure.

2. **The third democratic wave was not expected; and even during the wave, people doubted its advancement.**

   The end of Portugal's dictatorship in 1974 represented a step forward for democracy, but there was no assurance that this outcome would consolidate in Portugal itself, let alone begin a period of the largest democratic expansion in history. To the contrary, global trend lines at that time offered seemingly firm grounds for pessimism.

Labeling 1974 as "a grim time for freedom in the world," scholar Larry Diamond notes that in the prior year a coup had ended the Allende government in Chile.[43] Six years earlier, efforts to increase freedom in Czechoslovakia had been crushed by Soviet military power. The United States was in the process of disengaging from its tragic war in Vietnam. Laos and Cambodia would soon be overtaken by communist rule. Meanwhile, the US government was plagued by scandal in the Nixon administration. Diamond concludes: "In the mid-1970s, you had to be a crank or a romantic to believe that the bulk of the world's countries would become democratic over the next quarter century."[44]

Moreover, trends toward autocratization had been present for over a decade. Huntington notes: "In 1962, by one count, thirteen governments in the world were the product of coups d'état; by 1975, thirty-eight were. By another estimate one-third of thirty-two working democracies in the world in 1958 had become authoritarian by the mid-1970s."[45] He further observes that some transitions away from democracy during that time period had been particularly troubling, as states like

Chile, Uruguay, India, and the Philippines had sustained democratic governments for at least twenty-five years but still succumbed to authoritarianism.

Yet, Portugal (1974), and then Greece (1974-75), and Spain (1976-78) saw authoritarian governments fall and begin to transition to democracy, after which the wave began to advance in Latin America.

The wave's pace picked up after the 1986 "People Power" revolution in the Philippines ended the rule of dictator Ferdinand Marcos, followed by the democratic transition in South Korea, and then the end of the Pinochet regime in Chile in 1988. Yet the wave's biggest expansion was still to come with transitions among Soviet states between 1989 and 1991. This, too, was largely unforeseen.

Reflecting this point, scholar Timur Kuran quotes a 1989 Radio Free Europe broadcast stating: "Our jaws cannot drop any lower," regarding the fall of communist regimes in 1989.[46] In the face of popular uprisings and political transitions, Kuran observes that: "Wise statesmen, discerning diplomats, and gifted journalists were also caught off guard....As the *Economist* observed even before the East European Revolution had run its course, 1989 turned out to be a year when

Figure 2: Outcomes of Transitions from Authoritarianism According to Driver of the Transition (1972-2004)

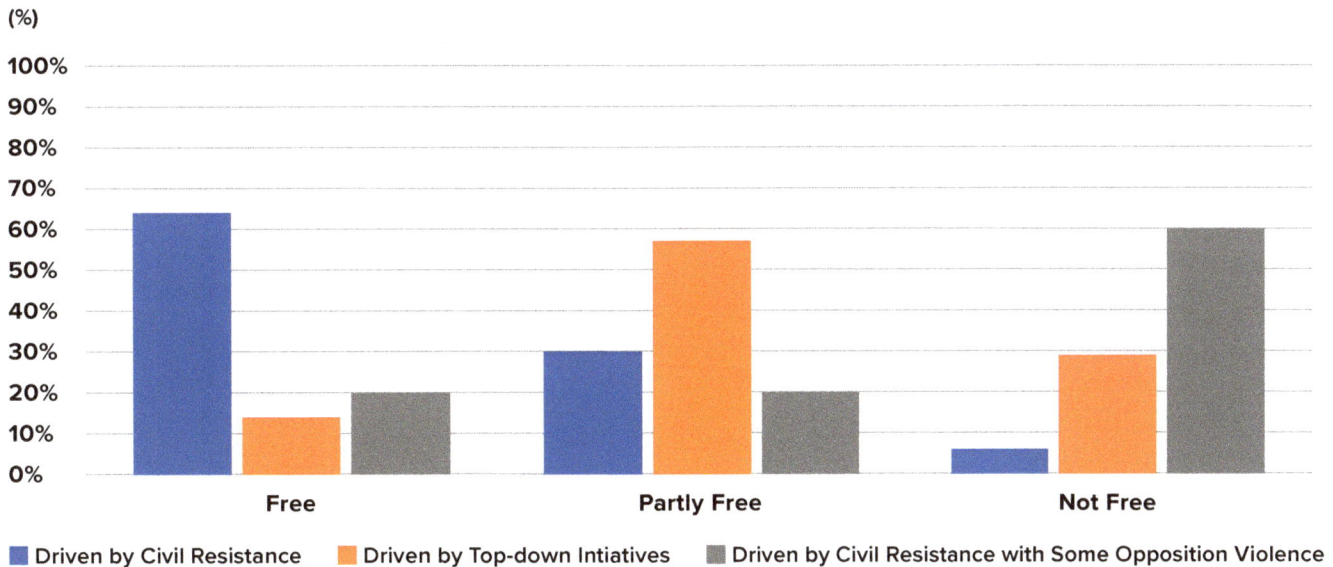

SOURCE: Adrian Karatnycky and Peter Ackerman, *How Freedom Is Won: From Civic Resistance to Durable Democracy*, (Washington, DC: Freedom House, 2005).

'the most quixotic optimists' were repeatedly 'proved too cautious.' "[47] Just a year prior, in September 1988, the CIA had predicted that the Eastern European regimes would continue.[48]

A final expansion of the third wave happened in the new century, and included popular revolutions in a number of former communist states. Scholar (and later Ambassador) Michael McFaul commented: "Another remarkable thing about these democratic break-throughs [in Serbia, Georgia, and Ukraine] is how few analysts predicted them."[49] He referred to how the toppling of Serbian dictator Milošević in 2000 seemed like a "miracle" to many, and stated that in Ukraine most observers in 2004 expected Yanukovich to be installed as the next president. He stated: "Not even opposition leaders predicted the scale and duration of the street protests" that would eventually lead to a democratic transfer of power.[50]

Implications for a fourth democratic wave: If a fourth wave rises, it is likely to occur in the face of democratic pessimism and doubts about the plausibility of such a wave. Therefore, working to foster a fourth wave likely will require a willingness to work in defiance of conventional wisdom and to argue for its prioritization amid competing policy priorities. To help forecast such a wave, it will also be necessary to give weight to indicators that are population- and movement-centered, as we discuss subsequently in this playbook.

3. **The third democratic and autocratic waves both started slowly.**

As it was developing in the 1970s, it was not evident that a third democratic wave was under way, and it proceeded slowly through the first decade. During this period, some states continued to break down into authoritarianism, even as others pushed toward democracy, and this resulted in only modest initial overall gains—the percentage of democratic states in the world increased from 30 percent to 34 percent between 1974 and 1982.[51] Pessimism about the prospect for democracy's spread remained until the mid-1980s.[52]

However, after a slow buildup over more than a decade, the wave's pace quickened significantly, catalyzed by civil resistance in places like the Philippines (1986), Chile (1988), Poland and Czechoslovakia (1989), the Baltic states and East Germany (1991), and South Africa (1992). Even when hardline elements sought to stop the democratization process in Russia, civil resistance prevented consolidation of a coup attempt in 1991.

Similar to the third democratic wave, the third autocratic wave started slowly, in the face of a false sense of confidence among democracies, and this created conditions conducive to its growth.[53] During its first decade after 2006, the wave tended to affect democracies gradually in ways that did not trigger consensus for vigorous action.[54] Thereafter, its implications became more apparent. For example, between 2016 and 2022, the number of people living in countries classified as "free" by the organization Freedom House declined from 39 percent of the world's population to 20 percent. Meanwhile, the number living in countries classified as "not free" rose from 36 percent to 39 percent.[55]

Implications for a fourth democratic wave: Fostering a fourth democratic wave will likely require sustained commitment, amid potentially ambiguous or slow initial results. Vision, persistence, and long-term planning without the need for constant short-term reinforcing feedback will likely be necessary.

4. **Quality of democracy matters for democratic durability.**

During past autocratic waves, new and electoral democracies have proven most susceptible to breakdown. (For a definition of electoral democracies, see the text box on page 26). Such breakdowns have happened even during democratic waves: for example, the beginning stages of the third autocratic wave have been identified as beginning in the mid-1990s, when a number of new electoral democracies failed to consolidate and began to backslide.[56]

While well-established liberal democracies are not immune to backsliding, especially during the third autocratic wave, they nonetheless remain more resilient overall than electoral democracies.[57]

Implications for a fourth democratic wave: A challenge in any democratic wave is to continue to support the consolidation process after a democratic transition. Focusing primarily on the presence of free and fair elections and basic democratic rights is not enough (such a misplaced focus has been referred to as the fallacy of "electoralism"), and leaves a country more susceptible to backsliding.[58] As Diamond notes:

*It is impossible for democracy to become consolidated when lawlessness reigns, corruption is rampant, and the state is weak. As Francis Fukuyama has stressed, **good governance**— or at least initially decent, as opposed to predatory, governance—is key to democracy's long-term prospects.[59] Badly governed, poorly performing democracies are accidents waiting to happen.[60]*

Zimbabwean lawyers carry placards as they march to demand justice for people detained in jail and others facing fast-track trials following recent protests in Harare, Zimbabwe, January 29, 2019. REUTERS/Philimon Bulawayo

Therefore, multiple measures of democracy and associated rights should be considered in determining the standards to which government elites are held, as well as for conditionality of aid, the forms of democracy assistance offered, and the length of time for which they are offered.

Moreover, even when a democratic transition happens under propitious circumstances, with well-designed institutions and economic growth occurring thereafter, democratic consolidation is also a function of time: the rules of the democratic game get more established with each iteration, over a number of election cycles. Accordingly, democracy assistance must be considered a long-term project, continuing well after democratic transitions.

5. Democratic diffusion and momentum matters.

Evidence from past democratic waves shows that democracy tends to develop and spread in geographic clusters. For example, based on data from 1816-1998, a country is more than five times as likely to be a democracy if the majority of its neighbors are democracies,

versus if the majority of its neighbors are nondemocracies.[61] Related research also finds that "countries tend to change their regimes to match the average degree of democracy or nondemocracy found among their contiguous neighbors."[62] Consistent with this, the presence of neighboring democracies is also found to help states remain resilient in the face of democratic backsliding.[63]

This points to a significant impact of regional democratic diffusion, as well as momentum that can be generated by recent democratic transitions in one or more countries within a region. On this point, scholars Kristian Skrede Gleditsch and Michael Ward find that:

The transition probabilities for a typical autocracy in a given year remain low, well below .015 [1.5 percent], when a small proportion of neighboring states are democracies...and there are no transitions in neighboring states. When the proportion of neighboring states exceeds one-half, however, the transition probabilities increase quite dramatically. The likelihood of a transition to democracy exceeds .10 [10 percent] when more than 75 percent of the neighboring states are democracies and is even higher when other countries in the region experience transitions to democracy.[64]

Notably, the above percentages apply per year, so a 10 percent predicted probability of transition in a given year would repeat annually as long as the relevant regional conditions hold.

However, regional context and diffusion can be a two-edged sword. For example, just as a higher number of democratic neighbors can make democratic transitions more likely, a higher number of authoritarian neighbors can make authoritarian regression more likely. Autocracies are also more likely to persist in regions with violent conflict than they are in regions of relative peace, and this creates incentives for them to foment violent instability.

Implications for a fourth democratic wave: A number of implications emerge from these lessons.

First, the authoritarian regimes that are most susceptible to democratic transitions tend to exist in relatively democratic neighborhoods, and a strategy that seeks to identify the most likely prospects for democratization may focus there.

Second, countries bordering and between predominantly democratic and authoritarian regions are likely to be active areas of contestation, and thus may merit significant strategic investment.

Third, when a country transitions to democracy in a relatively authoritarian neighborhood, that country becomes a potential new node from which further democratic development in the region can emanate. By definition then, such a country, regardless of size or other strategic interests, gains heightened geopolitical significance. However, such a country is also defying political gravity and is likely to regress to the regional mean for governance unless a foundation is built underneath it, which may necessitate significant and sustained support for its democratic transition.

Fourth, authoritarians currently have worldwide momentum on their side, and it is essential that this momentum be reversed. Doing so will require time, democratic solidarity, assertive strategy, and disciplined execution, but when these efforts swing momentum in the democratic direction, it is likely to form a positive feedback loop and generate ongoing collateral benefits.

6. **Civil resistance diffusion and momentum matters, if a movement is prepared to take advantage of them.**

As with diffusion of democratic transitions, there is also strong evidence that civil resistance movements can spread regionally to neighboring countries. In particular, movements are far more likely to spread to neighboring countries that have authoritarian regimes rather than those with democratic governments. This means that democratic governments are largely insulated from diffusion effects of civil resistance.[65]

Research also finds that the more democratic neighbors shared by an authoritarian regime, the higher the probability of diffusion of civil resistance to that regime.[66] One reason for this is because movements may use neighboring or nearby democratic countries as critical protected space to organize themselves and plan. For example, the *Otpor* (Resistance) movement in Serbia that ousted autocrat Milošević held meetings in Hungary. There is also evidence of regional diffusion of knowledge going beyond just neighboring countries. For example, Serbian activists traveled to Slovakia in 1998-99 to learn lessons from activists there, and Georgians and Ukrainians in turn learned lessons from Serbian activists.

Nonetheless, diffusion among civil resistance movements has not always led to positive outcomes: the Arab uprisings of 2010-11, for instance, did not yield major democratic gains in most countries. On this point, civil resistance in a neighboring country presents an opportunity as it can convey confidence and helpful information to populations, and undercut the confidence of an authoritarian regime's pillars of support. However, advance preparation is often critical to capitalize on this opportunity.

A key aspect of this preparation is development of clear leaders and movement infrastructures, which can process the implications of a neighboring civil resistance movement and then gauge and signal the timing for a population to engage in domestic mobilization. Without this, diffusion effects may manifest through thousands of individuals independently drawing quick inferences based on incomplete information (a process which may be catalyzed further by social media), and they may consequently overestimate the immediate vulnerability of their own regime and engage in a premature challenge.[67] Consistent with this view, rapid diffusion effects from civil resistance movements are found to be strongest in neighboring countries that have little recent history of mass mobilization (which can correspond to a lack of movement leaders and infrastructures). In contrast, countries with recent protest histories are more likely to pick the timing of their challenges based on domestic factors, and thus not rely as much on an immediate international trigger.[68]

Implications for a fourth democratic wave: Diffusion of civil resistance across borders represents an opportunity, but only when a movement is prepared. Therefore, support for movement organizing should happen well before a particular movement has emerged. Preparation and premobilization support (as we discuss subsequently in this playbook) is a critical and often-overlooked phase that ultimately sets a movement up to capitalize on opportunities, seize momentum of its own, and achieve success.

In addition, civil resistance diffusion largely affects authoritarian states, and tends to be much less likely in democratic states.

7. **Authoritarians are collaborating in the current autocratic wave.**

Far more than leaders of democratic countries, autocrats noticed the power of civil resistance, especially late in the third democratic wave. They watched Milošević fall in Serbia (2000), the Rose Revolution in Georgia (2003), and the Orange Revolution in Ukraine (2004). Feeling threatened, they observed, learned, strategized, and began to collaborate. Rulers from Russia, Belarus, China, Venezuela, Iran, Zimbabwe, and other countries began to speak pejoratively of these movements and their democratic breakthroughs as "color revolutions," falsely asserting they were a result of foreign-backed, regime-change efforts.

Concurrently, authoritarian regimes started sharing intelligence about these movements, strategies for repression, actual capacities (i.e., surveillance technology), and model legislation to suppress civil society.[69] In addition to the use of repressive public assembly laws and overbroad counterterrorism measures to limit public protests,[70] autocrats employed a range of other laws to stifle civil resistance movements, imposing serious civil and criminal sanctions if movement leaders engage in collective action without registering a formal organization. Legal restrictions on fundraising blocked movements' access to resources through laws barring informal groups from receiving donations from abroad or restricting the funding of formal civil society organizations, many of which support movements.[71] As movement organizers leveraged social media and other digital tactics to demand rights, governments responded with legal restrictions on speech and assembly online, as well as through

vague bans on online speech deemed "fake news" or harmful to national security.[72]

When these administrative and legal forms of repression fail, more overt forms of repression are applied. To this end, emergency transnational financing and agents of repression have been made increasingly available to bolster authoritarians being challenged by domestic movements.

A variety of international bribes, threats, and efforts at force projection also began to be used by authoritarians against nations, corporations, and individuals to try to silence democratic voices abroad and prevent actions that challenge autocratic states. Authoritarians further made efforts to shape the information environment internationally and within particular democratic societies; engaged in hacking and cyberattacks to interfere in democratic elections; funneled money to anti-democratic political groups; and in some cases militarily threatened or intervened against democracies, as with Ukraine, Georgia, and Taiwan.

While perpetrating these brazen abuses, authoritarians also spoke forcefully—and with profound hypocrisy—to advance a spurious norm of "hyper-sovereignty," functionally claiming that without consent of an authoritarian ruler, any support for popular movements, nongovernmental organizations, or human rights in general within their borders represents an unlawful violation of a nation's sovereignty.[73] Thus, authoritarians took free license to attack and undermine democratic states and brutally repress popular movements at will—including through cross-border violent tactics—but claimed that even modest efforts to bolster civil society in their countries represented impermissible intervention.

Moreover, throughout the course of the third autocratic wave, authoritarian collaboration has continued to deepen and increase. Illustrating how fearful authoritarians still are of their own populations, and how this draws them to form common cause, in 2022 Xi Jinping and Vladimir Putin released a high visibility joint statement of cooperation and took the trouble to note that:

Russia and China stand against attempts by external forces to undermine security and stability in their common adjacent regions, intend to counter interference by outside forces in the internal affairs of sovereign countries under any pretext, oppose colour revolutions, and will increase cooperation in the aforementioned areas.[74]

Implications for a fourth democratic wave: Years of international collaboration have provided autocrats with short-term and long-term offensive and defensive capabilities. Their offense involves a wide array of activities to propagate authoritarianism globally, project force to intimidate critics transnationally, and undermine democratic states. Defensive capabilities involve efforts to suppress civil society; repress nascent pro-democracy movements across borders; and increase international rapid-response capacities (including financial assistance and support for repressive capacities) to bolster authoritarian governments that are challenged by pro-democracy movements.

The net result is that each new pro-democracy movement around the world faces a coterie of authoritarians skillfully coordinating and aligned against it. Democratic states must respond by increasing their capacities for long-term engagement and rapid response capabilities to support these movements. They must also redouble efforts to address the legal repression faced by civil resistance movements by advocating for the reform of restrictive laws; helping movement members navigate legal restrictions; and providing protection through emergency legal and financial assistance to movement members who are targeted for their civic activism. Recognizing that too little support, arriving too late, may be as good as no support at all, strategic frameworks—such as the right to assistance outlined in this playbook—should also be developed to enable both proactive and responsive options, at times on short notice, to match the urgency of demands.[75]

8. **Democratic backsliding is a defining characteristic of the third autocratic wave, and is a major threat to the survival of democratic states.**

During the third autocratic wave, authoritarian governments have become more repressive, but much of the damage has occurred in democracies. The breadth of losses is extensive.[76] Over the last few decades, between 1993 and 2019, fifty-nine democracies began backsliding, and of these, thirty-six governments representing a total of over seven-hundred million people broke down into authoritarianism.[77]

More concerning still is that while historically democracies have proven effective at preventing the onset of backsliding, once the backsliding process starts (i.e., demagogues are elected and begin to dismantle the democratic system, amid toxic polarization), democracies have proven remarkably ineffective at countering it. An evaluation of the ninety-six episodes of democratic backsliding that occurred from 1900 to 2019 reveals that *nearly 68 percent broke down into authoritarian rule*. The ultimate percentage may be even higher, since

twelve backsliding episodes were still unresolved at the time of study and may also conclude in breakdown.[78]

Implications for a fourth democratic wave: Democratic backsliding is highly dangerous, and too often fatal for democratic countries. Yet it is also easy to underestimate this phenomenon because it tends to starts slowly and incrementally and is difficult to measure. This means that by the time a country has been publicly labeled as "backsliding," it is often already well on its way toward authoritarian breakdown.

Any effort to foster a fourth democratic wave must take this threat seriously, but should also note that democratic backsliding at home cannot be isolated from the undermining impacts of authoritarian regimes (including both their intentional attacks on democracies, and their negative diffusion effects), nor from backsliding abroad. Thus, fostering a fourth democratic wave requires an integrated strategy that:

- Strengthens democracy at home.

- Bolsters democratic resilience abroad.

- Internationally supports and enables democratic forces to challenge authoritarian regimes.

Privileging one of these emphases over the others sets up a false argument. Attention, resources, and an integrated strategy are needed to impact all of them.

9. **Civil resistance has become the prevailing means by which authoritarianism is countered, but has also suffered setbacks in the third autocratic wave.**

As the third autocratic wave grew from 2006 onward, civil resistance became a dominant means globally of directly challenging authoritarian regimes. Evidence also reveals its increasing use to demand political and economic reforms, including within democracies. We will address these two manifestations separately.

First, over the last few decades, the emergence of new "maximalist" civil resistance movements (seeking political transitions, self-determination or expulsion of foreign occupiers) grew significantly from the 1990s onward, as shown in Figure 3.[79]

Yet in spite of this rapidly rising incidence, the success rates of maximalist movements during the third autocratic wave have declined. From the high-water mark of 65 percent during the 1990s, success rates between 2010 and 2019 fell sharply to 34 percent,[80] as shown in Figure 4.

Figure 3: Onsets of Nonviolent and Violent Mass Campaigns, by Decade (1900-2019)

Campaign onsets per decade

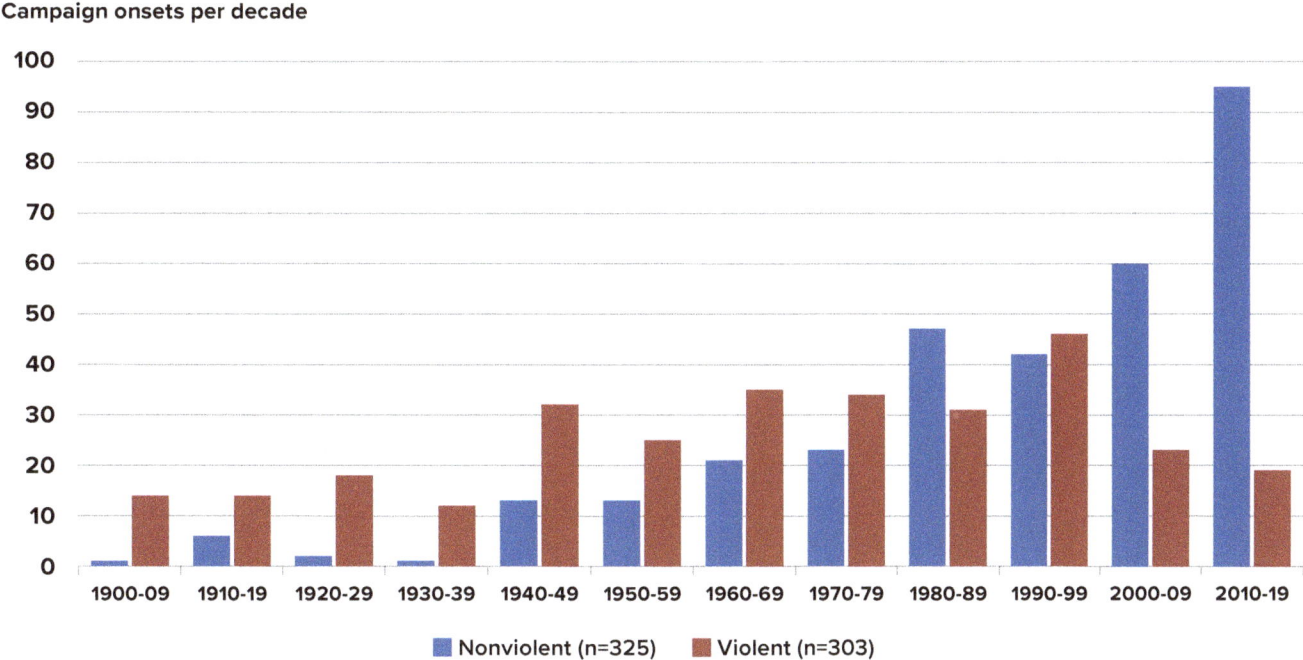

Nonviolent (n=325)   Violent (n=303)

SOURCE: Erica Chenoweth, "The Future of Nonviolent Resistance," *Journal of Democracy* 31, no. 3 (2020), 71.

Figure 4: Success Rates of Nonviolent and Violent Mass Campaigns, by Decade (1930-2019)

Success rates (%)

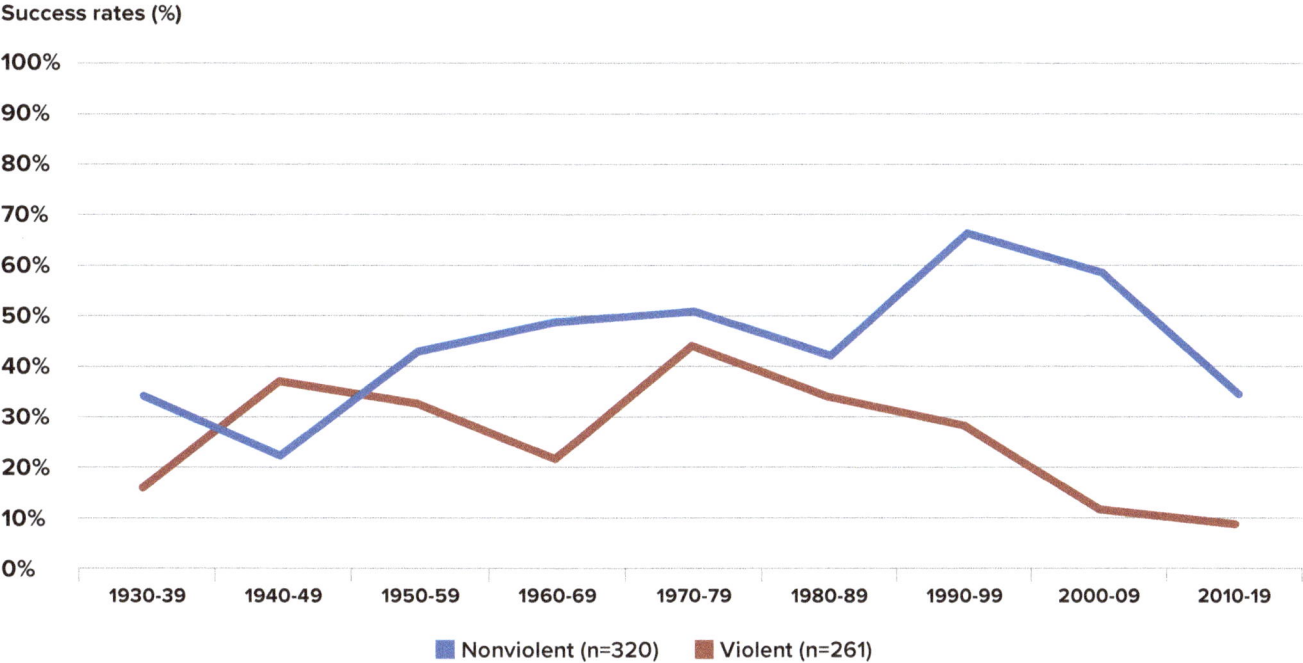

Nonviolent (n=320)   Violent (n=261)

SOURCE: Erica Chenoweth, "The Future of Nonviolent Resistance," *Journal of Democracy* 31, no. 3 (2020), 75.

A demonstrator uses a megaphone during a protest against Hungarian Prime Minister Viktor Orban and the latest anti-LGBTQ law in Budapest, Hungary, June 14, 2021. REUTERS/Marton Monus

Several interrelated factors are likely driving this trend. First, there is widespread consensus that new strategies, capacities, skills, and heightened solidarity among authoritarian governments have increased their abilities to repress popular mobilization. Second, there has not been a comparable investment in movements developing skills, strategies, capacities, and tactical innovations to counter the authoritarian resurgence. Third, movement overreliance on social media, overuse of protest demonstrations, and an increasing presence of violent flanks alongside movements have also likely dampened success rates.[81] Fourth, as a likely consequence of these factors, observed public participation in maximalist movements has declined by over 50 percent over two decades, as documented by scholar Erica Chenoweth:

In the 1980s, the average nonviolent campaign involved about 2 percent of the population in the country where it was underway. In the 1990s, the average campaign included a staggering 2.7 percent of the population. But since 2010, the average peak participation has been only 1.3 percent, continuing a decline that began in the 2000s. This is a crucial change. A mass uprising is more likely to succeed when it includes a larger proportion and a more diverse cross-section of a nation's population.[82]

Thus, the world is witnessing a growing number of movements challenging autocrats, but these movements have far lower average levels of public participation than in previous decades, as well as several other features that inhibit their success rates.

The use of civil resistance also has risen to demand reformist goals, including in democracies, although we do not have data solely dedicated to its use in democratic contexts. In lieu of this, it is possible to infer some conclusions from a comprehensive research study evaluating 2,809 incidents of civil resistance (ranging from hundreds to millions of participants) for a variety of causes in 101 countries (including democratic and authoritarian, in total comprising a total 93 percent of the global population) between 2006 and 2020.[83] The researchers found that since 2006, civil resistance has increased in every region of the world, and that the most common grievances and demands for which it is employed relate to:

- "Failure of political representation/political systems, focused on a lack of real democracy, corruption and other grievances" (54 percent).

- "Economic injustice and austerity reforms" (53 percent).

- "Civil rights, from indigenous/racial rights to women's rights and personal freedoms" (48 percent).

- "Global justice and a better international system for all" (30 percent).[84]

The researchers also found that 51 percent of civil resistance actions against provincial and local governments, and 43 percent of action against national governments, "resulted in some kind of demonstrable achievement, generally a partial success."[85] They contextualize this by noting that:

Success is rarely the result of one protest event alone, but the result of many years of protests focusing on the same grievance/demand....Many of the protests are engaged with long-term structural issues that may yield results in time; incremental or short-term achievements may prove to be precursors to more comprehensive change.[86]

In addition, despite their general use of the term "protests," the researchers find that other civil resistance tactics like strikes and boycotts tend to yield the highest success rates.

These results paint a somewhat more optimistic picture for civil resistance, where reform-based goals seem to be enjoying comparatively higher prospects of success, especially against local and provincial governments. Moreover, as the researchers note, the impact of civil resistance tactics can be iterative over time. Thus, incremental victories can add up, which can boost democratic resilience, as well as increase the skill base and confidence of a movement to achieve further gains.

Implications for a fourth democratic wave: A growing number of movements are using civil resistance to directly challenge authoritarian regimes, but over the past decade they have experienced a significant decline in success rates. Movements are also more frequently emerging to push for reformist goals such as greater government accountability, economic

fairness, and civil rights, including in democratic states. Evidence shows their ability to achieve incremental gains toward these ends, which can help to prevent democratic backsliding.

Democratic states are now faced with several urgent questions. First, can the current seventeen-year autocratic wave be countered if the success rates of movements seeking democratic transitions against authoritarian rule remain at a multidecade low? Second, what are the costs and risks of maintaining this status quo—leaving populations engaging in civil resistance to contend against a cabal of increasingly coordinated and aggressive authoritarian regimes? Third, what are the options for increasing movement support, and what are their accordant risks?

Research finds that civil resistance movements are historically one of the most powerful drivers of democratic gains worldwide. Consistent with this, we foresee no scenario for a fourth democratic wave in which movements do not play a central role. With authoritarians collaborating, and movement success rates declining, the risks of relative inaction by democracies on this front have become unacceptable.

We also recognize that engaging with movements can be complex, and entail its own risks. However, these can be mitigated through investments in improved government capacities and decision-making in this area. Doing so represents one of the greatest and most overlooked opportunities available internationally today. The societies ruled by authoritarians are critical domains of contention, and authoritarians clearly remain vulnerable, as evidenced by their insatiable demand to repress their populations. Demagogues in backsliding democracies also target civil society for the same reason. They would not do this if they felt confident.

The critical issue is how to best engage with the millions of allies who can lead the fight (it is first and foremost their fight) for democracy and human rights in their home countries.

The rest of the playbook offers a strategy to contend on this front.

PART 2

A Three-Pillar Strategy to Foster a Fourth Democratic Wave

3. Pillar I: Broadening Options to Enable and Support Civil Resistance

There are two aspects to government support to civil resistance movements.

The first relates to development of an overall foreign policy that conveys greater recognition and weight to democracy as a key national interest, and incorporates democracy support and countering authoritarianism into decisions across all elements of state power.[87]

The second is through efforts that focus specifically on movement support. One option to do so is through a variety of public programs that share information across borders about how civil resistance can advance democracy and human rights. Another way is through diverse forms of direct engagement with particular movements in countries around the world. Democracies can also collaborate to impose greater costs when authoritarian regimes engage in repression.

As stated in the previous chapter, movement support can be complex and entail risk, but this can be navigated by developing improved government capacities and decision-making. We note that nearly two decades ago, authoritarians began to make comprehensive investments in how to suppress civil resistance movements. Their incremental and multifaceted efforts built cumulatively year after year. It is overdue for democratic governments to take a similar long-term approach to engage on this front, as part of a broader democracy-centered foreign policy.

We address these aspects in further detail below.

A Democracy-Centered Foreign Policy

The backbone of movement support is a democracy-centered foreign policy. Well-organized civil resistance movements use every bit of political space available to them. International support for freedoms of expression, assembly, association, press, and other human rights—as well as substantial pressure on regimes that violate these freedoms—creates an enabling environment for these movements. In turn, on their own initiative, these movements can then more effectively push for changes that enable a democracy-centered foreign policy to succeed.

Such a policy would recognize that protecting and supporting democracy is a key national interest, and also that our definition of democracy *must be bound with human rights*. As Huntington observes:

> Liberal democracies not only have elections. They also have restrictions on the power of the executive; independent judiciaries to uphold the rule of law; protection for individual rights and liberties of expression, association, belief, and participation; consideration for the right of minorities; limits on the ability of the party in power to bias the electoral process; effective guarantees against arbitrary arrest and police brutality; no censorship; and minimal government control of the media.[88]

Accordingly, governments that hold elections but antagonize civil society should not be given a pass, since closing civic space is synonymous with democratic backsliding. On this point, Diamond remarks that "we cannot win the struggle for democracy unless we also wage a vigorous struggle for liberty and human rights."[89]

While policymakers consider a broad range of important national and strategic interests, including trade and security cooperation, prioritizing democracy and human rights in their decision-making is essential for the achievement of critical long-term goals. This calls for a careful reassessment and rebalancing of state interests and their relative weight in decision-making.

The United States has done this before, with impressive results. More than four decades ago, the world witnessed the power of a popular nonviolent uprising by the Solidarity movement in Poland in 1980-81. Around this same time, arguments began to be made that human rights should be elevated on the US foreign policy agenda. For example, in a 1981 confidential memorandum, senior officials at the State Department pressed the case:

> "Human Rights"—meaning political rights and civil liberties—gives us the best opportunity to convey what is ultimately at issue in our contest with the Soviet bloc. The fundamental difference between us is not in economic or social policy, but in our attitudes toward freedom. Our ability to resist the Soviets around the world depends in part on our ability to draw this distinction and persuade others of it.[90]

On the question of balancing competing national interests, they wrote:

> We have to be prepared to pay a price. In most *specific cases taken alone, the need for good bilateral relations will seem to outweigh our broad concerns for freedom and decency. Nevertheless, it is a major error to subordinate these considerations in each case—because* **taken together** *these decisions will destroy our policy....If we act as if offenses against freedom don't matter in countries friendly to us, no one will take seriously our words about Communist violations.*

They conclude by arguing that:

> A human rights policy means trouble, *for it means hard choices which may adversely affect certain bilateral relations....There is no escaping this without destroying the policy, for otherwise what would be left is simply coddling friends and criticizing foes. Despite the costs of such a real human rights policy,* **it is worth doing and indeed it is essential.**[91]

As these points began to hold sway, the US Congress, with bipartisan support, established the National Endowment for Democracy. In ensuing years, the US government provided greater weight to human rights in certain personnel and policy decisions; pulled back from dictators like Augusto Pinochet and Ferdinand Marcos at key moments when they were challenged by popular pro-democracy movements; and supported broadcasters like Voice of America and Radio Free Europe/Radio Liberty to provide a counterpoint to dictators' censorship and propaganda. These actions and policies are credited with playing a role in the end of the Cold War and concurrent expansion of the third democratic wave.[92]

A Movement Support Strategy

The second aspect of government support relates to specific forms of engagement with movements. The very qualities that make movements resilient and powerful also can make them challenging to assist. Movements tend to be somewhat fluid, depend on widespread voluntary participation, can operate in highly repressive environments, and have varying degrees of structure or organization. Thus, navigating questions of external assistance related to "when," "what," "how," and "to whom" begins with cultivating a movement mindset: understanding what to look for, how to discern needs, and how to engage accordingly based on different contexts.[93] There is no simple formula, but past experience and research allow us to identify best practices and guideposts to orient external supporters to this vital task.

Several insights offer baselines in this regard.

The first is that external support should be seen as an extension of—rather than a substitute for—a movement developing the necessary domestic participation, organization, attributes, and strategy to win on the ground. The movement is the primary actor, with enormous potential leverage within its country, knowledge of its local context, and the most at stake in the conflict.

This sentiment is echoed consistently in the research literature on civil resistance. For example, a broad-based study on movement support finds that "both quantitative and qualitative evidence suggest that external support is always secondary to local actors."[94] A United States Institute of Peace evidence review titled "External Support for Nonviolent Action" echoes this view:

> The principles of humility and "do no harm" should...be primary values for all those interested in supporting nonviolent action. External supporters are not the protagonists of the story. They are secondary characters. They may play a key role at certain moments, but they should never forget the primary actors who will have the greatest impact on the campaign's outcome and for whom the stakes of the nonviolent campaign are the highest.[95]

Emerging from this point, **a second insight is that external actors should actively solicit movement requests for assistance, support local ownership and empowerment, and be flexible as local partners determine how best to apply the support received.**

Among the wide range of possible forms of external support—from training, to offering funding, to condemnations of repression, to sanctions against authoritarian governments—research has found that most of these options can have a range of effects depending on context.[96] Therefore, it is best to defer to the judgment of those who know their local circumstances best. For example depending on the case, various economic sanctions have helped movements (i.e., the anti-apartheid movement in South Africa), hindered them, and had negligible or ambiguous impacts. Likewise, certain forms of funding have helped movements in some cases (i.e., Serbia 1998-2000), but fed movement infighting (i.e., Belarus 2006) and heightened government repression in others. One notable exception to this is that among all forms of external support, providing various forms of training has been found to have consistently positive effects—which is a topic addressed in greater detail below.

Based on these findings, seeking to impose external agendas on movements, or even providing well-intentioned support without consultation with local groups, can risk unintended negative consequences. If a movement starts carrying the agenda of a foreign supporter, for example, it may become a target for heightened regime repression, lead to infighting, or result in domestic supporters no longer mobilizing on its behalf.

A third insight from research and past experience is that the impact of movement support can be strengthened when external parties coordinate.[97]

Movements have a wide range of needs that may change over time. Governments, international nongovernmental organizations (advocacy and philanthropy), diaspora groups, multilateral organizations, and transnational solidarity networks can all play support roles, and each has comparative advantages in respective areas. Therefore, as governments consider options to better collaborate among themselves, they should also consider partnerships with other allies in their movement support efforts.

Building from these baselines, there is a large amount that external supporters can do to help movements achieve democratic goals. Different frameworks can be helpful in navigating these decisions, and below we apply one based on five movement phases, during which movements experience different challenges, opportunities, and needs. While not all five phases apply to every movement, they represent common themes across different contexts. The phases are:

1. Early organizing.

2. Peak mobilization.

3. Protracted struggle.

4. Transition.

5. Post-transition.

Activities in the "early organizing" and "peak mobilization" stages are fundamental to shaping the movement's trajectory and subsequent prospects for success, and therefore we focus predominantly on considerations for external support during these first two phases.

PHASE 1: EARLY ORGANIZING

In the early organizing phase, activists and organizers aim to form a movement or a small movement has already formed, but largely remains outside of public view. At this critical point, appropriate external assistance can make a major impact with relatively small investment. This also may be one of the only periods in a movement's lifespan in which time is a plentiful resource. Yet most external actors fail to recognize early organizing as an oppor-

tunity for support, and instead tend to pay attention to movements only at later phases (i.e., once the movement encounters public repression).

The challenges and opportunities faced by movements in the early organizing phase include convening and training to develop a core of leaders; strategic assessment and planning for *all* remaining phases of the movement (through even the post-transition phase); increasing public awareness about the prospect of civil resistance; building unity among supporters for shared goals and a positive vision; and relationship and trust building with representatives of key groups that will enable the movement to increase mobilization when it is ready.

Key support activities for external actors during this phase include the following: training and capacity building, support for public education campaigns on civil resistance, fostering unity and widespread participation, technology support, and financial assistance.

Training and Capacity Building

Research on external support to movements strongly validates the importance and impact of educational, training, and skill-building efforts. A recent comprehensive study finds that "training seems to effectively support nonviolent campaigns more consistently than any other form of assistance" and that:

> *Activists who receive training prior to peak mobilization are much more likely to mobilize campaigns with high participation, low fatalities, and greater likelihood of [security force] defections.*[98]

Training is also "associated with a lower propensity for a campaign to adopt or tolerate a violent flank."[99]

Training and capacity building help activists learn valuable information, strategize, and apply knowledge of civil resistance in their local context. Support for planning workshops and the development of movement-specific educational resources also provide opportunities for activists to deepen their skills and coordination.[100]

The strategic planning process begins with an assessment of the nascent movement, its opponent, and the domestic and international operating environment. From this analysis, the movement can identify strengths and weaknesses of itself and its opponent, opportunities and risks, potential allies, and long- and short-term objectives to increase its internal capacity and wage conflict. External actors can sometimes further help movements in this process by researching and offering information about the composition and relationships of regime pillars of support and regime enablers, and by identifying financial flows and other key relationships from which the regime draws its power.

Activists can then begin to develop specific campaign plans to achieve intermediate goals. Devising innovative tactics, concentrating movement strengths against an opponent's weaknesses, and sequencing tactics to increase social, political, and economic pressure are all aspects of this process.

Strategic planning facilitators should also challenge activists to think through the entire course of their struggle. Too frequently, movements grow quickly—beyond the expectations of their originators—but then lack a strategy and structure to continue to push toward victory. For example, a movement may rapidly move to peak mobilization, but then have no plan for phases afterward—i.e., protracted struggle, transition, or post-transition—that require different strategies and competencies. Therefore, the time for a movement to plan for a political transition is well *before* it engages in mass mobilization. What would a transition and post-transition process look like? By what mechanism would the transition happen—the legislature passing a new law, winning an election, negotiations, resignation of an autocrat, or some combination? How long would the transition process be? What stages would it have? Who would have a seat at the negotiating table? What essential elements of the current regime must change? Are there certain elements that must remain? How would accountability and transitional justice for past perpetrators of abuse be handled? It takes time to examine and build consensus on possible answers to these questions, and time becomes an increasingly scarce resource after the early organizing phase progresses to the peak mobilization.

As movements develop their goals and strategies, they will also want to identify metrics so they can determine their progress over time. "Is the dictator still in power?" or "Has the terrible law been repealed yet?" are the default indicators many movements use, and unfortunately relying primarily on such indicators provides little guidance to assess a movement's prospects and next steps. Instead, indicators based on the status of key movement attributes and dynamics can provide a more helpful basis for analysis through all phases of a conflict (see the text box on movement metrics on the next page for examples).

Lastly, based on the above comprehensive analysis, movement organizers can develop practices and principles by which their movement will operate, spread, and become publicly identified, and to which all new movement participants must agree. A movement is like an organism, and its internal practices, principles, and culture are like its DNA. As a movement grows, it becomes impossible to command and control hierarchically, and the movement DNA serves as a basis for ongoing unity. It provides guidance for local groups to organize themselves, plan, and engage in tactics that align with the movement's overall goals and strategy. Addressing this matter at a movement's inception is critical—launching mass mobilization *without* first intentionally developing movement DNA creates a weakness that can be highly challenging to address subsequently.

In terms of who organizes and leads strategic planning support activities, nonstate actors—international nongovernmental organizations (advocacy, philanthropy), civil society organizations (CSOs), or diaspora groups—are generally the best conveners, and governments may support such organizations financially or through other means (i.e., in-kind contributions) to hold workshops in person or online. In keeping with the principle of deferring to local actors, it is also important for trainers to understand that their role is to facilitate and share knowledge, rather than to deliver advice. External actors can share case studies, research findings, and planning tools as well as engage in Socratic dialogue with activists about prioritizing various tactics, but they should not advocate for particular courses of action. However, a single exception to this is that external actors should feel comfortable advising against the use of violence. Violent insurgency is empirically proven to be a disastrous choice for populations, and the strategic advantages of nonviolent tactics are established in research and practice.[101]

Support for Public Education Campaigns on Civil Resistance

Dissidents rising up against oppression face the choice of whether to employ violent or nonviolent tactics. As they encounter increasing threat, they are likely to choose the form of resistance that seems most powerful to them. Too often they erroneously perceive violence as their most potent option.[102]

In this circumstance, calling for peace and criticizing violence are effective only if a viable alternative means of struggle is offered.[103] Public education efforts can spread awareness that civil resistance is a powerful force for democracy and human rights, with a much higher success rate than violence.[104]

In addition, civil resistance has far broader appeal than violence. Nonviolent movements can enlist the support and participation of a wide demographic (men, women, parents, elders, youth and others), whereas violence is

Movement Metrics

Drawing from the work of civil resistance experts Peter Ackerman and Hardy Merriman, we highlight four key attributes and three trends associated with movement success that may be tracked over time.[*]

Movement Attributes

Unity: Indicators include coalition growth, growing diversity of groups represented in mobilization, and agreement on leadership and a positive vision for the future.

Strategic planning capacity: Indicators include tactical innovation, tactical sequencing, clear and strategic campaign goals, and the establishment of an active training program for activists.

Maintenance of nonviolent discipline: Indicators include the ability to remain nonviolent even in the face of provocations, statements of leaders calling for nonviolent conduct, and mandatory training for new movement participants on the need for nonviolent discipline.

A plan to consolidate a democratic outcome: Indicators include the presence of a transition and post-transition plan, the establishment of regular assessments, updates of that plan, and widespread support for that plan.

Trends

Increasing civilian participation: Indicators include growing numbers of movement participants.

Diminishing impact of repression and increasing backfire: Indicators include repression failing to demobilize movement participants, or actively increasing mobilization and support for the movement (domestically, and sometimes also internationally).

Increasing defections from a movement's adversary: Indicators include public defections by members of a regime's pillars of support (i.e., security services, bureaucrats, state-allied media, judiciary, economic elites, or others) and/or evidence of decreased state capacity due to subtle loyalty shifts (defections that are not public, but manifest as shirking responsibility and decreased efficiency).

Ultimately, movements must define their own metrics, but the above list can serve as a starting point for discussion.

*SOURCE: PETER ACKERMAN AND HARDY MERRIMAN, "THE CHECKLIST FOR ENDING TYRANNY," IN *IS AUTHORITARIANISM STAGING A COMEBACK?*, EDS. MATHEW BURROWS AND MARIA J. STEPHAN (WASHINGTON, DC: ATLANTIC COUNCIL, 2015), 63-79; AND PETER ACKERMAN, *THE CHECKLIST TO END TYRANNY: HOW DISSIDENTS WILL WIN 21ST CENTURY CIVIL RESISTANCE CAMPAIGNS*, (WASHINGTON, DC: ICNC PRESS, 2022).

often marketed narrowly to men and sometimes women of fighting age. Accordingly, Chenoweth finds, "The average nonviolent campaign is about eleven times as large (as a proportion of the population) than the average violent campaign."[105] There are also much lower barriers to enter a civil resistance campaign than a violent insurgency.[106] People may participate in a boycott, protest, or other acts of subtle or overt noncooperation and then return to their everyday lives, whereas violent insurgents often have to make enormous and sometimes irreversible changes to their lives based on their chosen form of struggle.[107]

These and many other points gleaned from scholarship, practice, and case accounts (preferably drawn from the region in question) can be communicated through public information campaigns and institutions such as schools, universities, neighborhood associations, labor unions, religious bodies, and youth clubs. They can be customized to draw on a society's history, values, and appropriate terminology, and can be expressed through diverse means such as literature, videos, films, television shows, news media, advertisements, music, public performances, visual art, cultural practices, social media, popular events, and statements by respected leaders.[108]

Public education efforts also can be supported through underwriting research about best practices and case studies of civil resistance, developing and sharing general educational resources on this topic, and translating resources into languages spoken around the world.[109]

Moreover, a wide range of external actors—from governments and international nongovernmental organizations to diaspora populations—can potentially play a role in such efforts. Public education activities avoid potential political problems with supporting a particular movement or outcome, and instead have the general purpose of making knowledge available, attractive, and accessible to all.[110]

Fostering Unity and Widespread Participation

Mutual understanding, relational ties, and trust are catalysts that enable coalitions and movement leadership to form and function. However, divide and rule is a cornerstone of the authoritarian playbook, which means that most movements face the challenge of unifying diverse groups and factions in society.

External actors can help movements build unity by offering and maintaining safe meeting spaces, and creating sustained processes to promote dialogue among members of fragmented opposition groups. As one historical example, the British Foreign Office convened elements of the Serbian opposition in 1999 to foster unity, which both strengthened the pro-democracy movement during times of contestation, as well as its ability to effectively foster a political transition.[111]

There are at least three aspects in this process that can be supported.

Unity of Purpose

It is often easier for a movement to agree on a negative vision (what it stands against) than to agree to a positive vision of what it stands for. Yet the development of a positive vision and goals are critical for maintaining longer-term cohesion, resisting authoritarian attempts to sow division, inoculating against disinformation, and consolidating a movement's gains. Waiting to begin conversations about unity of purpose until the peak mobilization phase—as sometimes happens when a public outrage triggers mass demonstrations—is much more challenging than addressing this issue in the early organizing phase.

Developing unity on strategy is also important among a movement's initiators, and this can be accomplished through their involvement in strategic planning work-

shops. Once the movement is launched, a well-conceived strategy will continue to gain supporters over time, as the movement's gains convince skeptics and fence-sitters that the movement can win.

Unity on Leadership

Movements that develop both centralized and decentralized leadership structures are formidable adversaries against even violent authoritarian regimes. Decentralized leadership fosters resilience to repression and enables local tactical decision-making. Centralized leadership fosters long-term planning and an easier ability to negotiate with potential allies and regime defectors.

However, overreliance on one or the other form of leadership within movements becomes a liability that can exploited. Overcentralization risks that leaders, who can be arrested or possibly co-opted, become the only basis for unity or strategic direction to the movement. Centralized leaders also can lose touch with their grassroots base, blunder at the negotiating table, or begin to engage in political rivalries and infighting as they seek to position themselves for a possible future political transition.

On the other hand, relying only on decentralized organizing (which some refer to as a "leaderless," or alternatively, "leaderful" approach) can make it difficult for a movement to engage in long-term planning. Negotiations—both among potential allies and with potential defectors from the regime's support base—also become more challenging to conduct. Thus, exclusive reliance on decentralization can help a movement withstand repression and grow in one phase of its development, but then impede its development and maturation in later phases.

While movements benefit from both forms of leadership, they are not necessarily needed equally at the same time. Having public leaders may not be essential at a movement's inception, and sometimes leaders emerge through the course of a movement. Regardless, the questions of "Who will represent us?" and/or "How will we determine who represents us?" must be considered at a movement's outset and continue throughout its growth.

Unity of People

Research identifies diverse and high levels of public participation as one of the most important contributors to movement success. Widespread popular mobilization enables a movement to exert simultaneous pressures on its opponent through a range of tactics, at various targets, in rapid sequence. In addition, high and diverse levels of participation give a movement more contact points with its opponent's supporters—i.e., people who work in the state bureaucracy, security forces, judiciary, economic entities, state-aligned media, and other institutions—which can help the movement to foster defections within those sectors.

Evidence also suggests the powerful impact that some specific groups of participants can have on movements. For example, Chenoweth's research finds that higher degrees of frontline participation by women, as well as the participation of formal women's organizations in movements, both correlate with heightened movement success rates. High degrees of women's frontline participation as well as calls by women's organizations to engage in peaceful resistance are also associated with fewer breakdowns into violence by movements, and with a heightened probability of defections among regime security forces.[112]

A further study on the role of women and youth in movements, published by the United States Institute of Peace (USIP), finds that their participation increases a movement's tactical innovation, nonviolent discipline, and coalition opportunities (i.e., mobilization across numerous groups). Notably, women and youth also represent a massive portion of many countries' populations. However, they also can experience certain barriers to movement participation, including gendered forms of repression, economic precarity, and cultural norms that inhibit their rise to leadership. This means that extra efforts may be needed to reach out to, listen to, and engage with these powerful movement actors.[113]

Participation by organized labor groups can also be a potent catalyst, and their participation is associated with higher movement success rates and subsequent democratization. Between 1946 and 2006, nearly 83 percent of "maximalist" civil resistance movements that included national trade unions were successful, but only approximately 29 percent succeeded without this participation. National trade union participation also increases the magnitude of democratic gains after a movement succeeds. These benefits may reflect the fact that unions have significant economic leverage on regimes, can increase overall movement participation, and retain sufficient structure to be able to negotiate and lock in gains in the post-transition period.[114]

These examples illustrate that each group brings their own skills, capacities, and networks to a movement, which can increase the movement's strength and tactical options.

Yet how is such diverse and broad participation achieved?

Mobilization depends in large part on trust and linkages between groups, and these attributes may historically already exist, or may need to be intentionally cultivated in the early organizing phase. A movement can be understood as a network of relationships, which may lie dormant or publicly hidden, until such time as they are activated in mobilization. Therefore, by intentionally cultivating broader and deeper ties among different groups in the early organizing phase, a movement increases its *mobilization potential*, which can later manifest as heightened public participation (*actualized mobilization*).[115]

This process of building unity requires time, rapport, and resources. External actors can help with resources, and sometimes also by building bridges between groups.[116]

Technology Support

A movement's technology use should be considered intentionally in the early organizing phase. This entails analysis of both international trends and local context.

Globally, information technology is an increasingly important domain in any struggle between movements and authoritarian regimes. Yet early optimism about technology's liberating potential has given way to the reality that many regimes are winning this battle—increasing censorship, surveillance, propaganda, and misinformation while effectively curtailing activists from reaping many of technology's earlier benefits. This slanted playing field is most pronounced in fully authoritarian regimes—with the Chinese government's digital totalitarianism as the most extreme example—and each year authoritarians collaborate worldwide and upgrade their repressive technological capacities (in some cases they do so with support of technology exports from democracies, which must stop).[117] In contrast, among backsliding democracies, the internet remains more open to varying degrees, but demagogues continue to try to build their advantage by using digital tools.

These regime efforts all impact movements and have enabled autocrats to lower their risks of engaging in repression. Of particular importance to activists is the way that regimes engage in increasingly preemptive and "smart" forms of repression.[118] Based on the trove of information about domestic populations available to them, and sophisticated algorithms and artificial intelligence with which to analyze this data, authoritarians are able to more easily flag and monitor early signs of dissent, and quickly move to repress individuals or small groups that then never have an opportunity to grow. Such repression is highly impactful but often hidden or not widely visible, and therefore minimizes risk of backfire or defections against the regime.[119]

People hold white sheets of paper in protest over ongoing zero-COVID restrictions, as well as restrictions of freedom of speech and expression, on November 28, 2022 in Beijing, China. REUTERS/Thomas Peter

In addition, activists sometimes compound these problems by using technology in nonstrategic ways. For example, the mobilization potential of social media is well documented, but mobilization without organization has proven fleeting and fosters subsequent disillusionment. Activist overreliance on technology for communications and network coordination has led to increased opportunities for government surveillance. Inadequate security precautions heighten the risk of infiltration. Technological engagement also can lead activists to prioritize metrics (i.e., views, clicks) that sidetrack them from more important activities.

It is against this backdrop that movements and external actors must assess what problems technology solves for civil resistance, what problems it creates, and what the potential risk/reward ratio is of using or depending on various technological platforms and functions. Different contexts will yield different answers, and customization of technological solutions that fit purpose and local context are key. There are a number of ways external actors can help movements in this regard.

First, as with all forms of external assistance, external actors should seek out activists, ask them what they need, and listen to them. In addition to helping tailor support to local contexts, some external actors have capacities to develop new tools (including potentially those that can operate autonomously of regime-controlled/monitored internet) in the short or long term that can help to shift the slanted technological playing field back into activists' favor.

Second, external actors can help movements to analyze their country's specific profile for technology. Each society has different platforms, infrastructure, laws, user behaviors, and government capacities. Understanding these allows movements to make informed judgments in the early organizing phase about how they will use technology strategically, and the extent to which they will rely on it for various movement functions. In this assessment, the importance of metrics identified earlier in this chapter should be emphasized, with the aim that technology should be used to bolster attributes and dynamics that are proven to increase movement success rates.

Third, external actors can stress multiyear time horizons for change, and emphasize the crucial cultivation of offline forms of connection and organizing. Through in-person communities and networks—workplaces, trade unions, houses of worship, cultural convenings, schools, and recreational groups—movements can potentially deepen relationships and communicate without relying on the internet. (Notably, many movements succeeded against autocratic regimes before the modern internet or smartphones existed). Likewise, external actors can provide technical assistance and support for movements to develop functional redundancy in communications, organizing, and other operations, so that activists do not depend solely on vulnerable online platforms that the regime can curtail.

Fourth, external actors can provide security training to activists, which should be based on the technological profile of the specific country and its population. Such training should happen regularly, both to reinforce its lessons and to account for rapidly changing circumstances.

Fifth, one of the most powerful uses of technology for activists is often education and training. Online platforms to connect activists to training opportunities, coaching, videos, and educational materials are opportunities that external actors may want to leverage—with proper emphasis on digital security.

Sixth, external actors can support movement-adjacent efforts related to technology, such as supporting local media, international media, and efforts to combat misinformation, which help to create an enabling environment for movements.[120] Backsliding democracies in particular may offer significant opportunities to localize such activities.

Seventh, external actors should call attention to preemptive repression, which is often a result of digital surveillance, and attempt to raise its cost for regimes. The names, faces, and stories of victims must be publicized; perpetrators and enablers must be named; the repression's impact must be made public; and it must be framed as a broader pattern of human rights abuse. Punitive action should be considered against perpetrators and enablers. External actors may also help activists cultivate links to the engineers that build and maintain structures of digital authoritarianism, to help foster their defection (which may be highly consequential) or to impose social, economic, or political costs on them.[121]

Lastly, democracies should refuse to export technologies used for repression, which is a topic addressed in Pillar III (chapter 5).

Financial Assistance

Some of the aforementioned forms of assistance—training, convenings, offering certain technology support—can involve relatively modest amounts of funding to reach grassroots actors. In addition, some activists may request funding to support local organizations to build the movement's resource base, recruit and train new participants, develop new strategies, and coordinate efforts among different locales.[122]

While these requests are not necessarily resource intensive, any form of funding to movements must be approached with caution, and especially by government donors. Movements are generally not designed to absorb, manage, and allocate significant amounts of external material resources. Therefore, the downside risks of providing direct funding include inducing infighting within a movement, supporting nongovernmental organizations that inadvertently siphon talent away from a movement's grassroots leadership, distorting local engagement and agendas that weaken movement credibility, and fueling regime accusations that damage the movement's legitimacy and serve as a pretext for repression.[123] Consistent with this, scholars Chenoweth and Maria Stephan find that on average:

> *Direct funding to movements has few generalizable effects on movement characteristics or outcomes. The only statistically significant finding suggests that direct financial assistance to movements is correlated with fewer participants in the campaign, suggesting it has adverse effects on a vital movement characteristic.[124]*

However, there are ways that these risks can be reduced. These include offering in-kind contributions, issuing funding in small installments, creating more activist-friendly grant practices (with lower administrative burdens and flexible reporting requirements), intentionally coordinating funding among donors, and allowing intermediaries (international governmental organizations, CSOs, and diaspora groups) with deep subject matter expertise (i.e., civil resistance training) or knowledge of the local context to guide funding.[125]

Funding also can be provided to more structured movement-adjacent organizations, which may help the movement achieve its goals indirectly. For example, external support (which can include funding or other forms of assistance) to local media is associated with lower movement fatalities and increasing likelihoods of security force defections and movement success.[126] Likewise, support to labor groups "is correlated with higher participation, non-violent discipline, and security force defections."[127] Lastly, support to opposition political parties is correlated with increased nonviolent discipline, movement participation, and success rates.[128]

PHASE 2: PEAK MOBILIZATION

In the peak mobilization phase, movements trigger public confrontation with their opponents.[129] They now seek to make their *actualized mobilization* match the *mobilization potential* that they developed in the early organizing phase. As the movement's visibility rises, it starts to face targeted repression.

Challenges and opportunities in the peak mobilization phase involve making repression backfire, maintaining nonviolent discipline in the face of regime provocations, and inducing defections from a regime's pillars of support.

External actors can support movements during this phase by taking several actions: mitigating the impacts of repression and disruption, supporting nonviolent discipline, supporting ongoing strategy development, and fostering defections. In addition, external actors can play a powerful role at this stage by raising the costs of movement repression through imposing sanctions, monitoring, and condemnations, and withdrawal of support from authoritarian regimes. We discuss these latter options in Pillar III (chapter 5) of this strategy, which focuses on how external actors can deter and constrain authoritarian regimes.

Mitigating the Impacts of Repression and Disruption

Disruption is inevitable when a movement challenges a government and can take the form of lost wages or scarcity of goods and services, for example. In such cases, outsiders can provide remediation options. When activists engage in labor strikes, the ability to quickly mobilize and support strike funds to mitigate household suffering—as was done when US and European labor unions provided support for strikes by Solidarity in Poland in the 1980s—is a relatively small investment that may have potentially high returns. External actors can also provide medical services via facilities inside the country or via sanctuaries outside the country.[130]

In addition, when activists are subject to repression, providing greater access to urgent and emergency support services—including legal, security, health, communication, financial, and (in worst-case scenarios) family relocation support—can make a difference.[131]

Supporting Nonviolent Discipline

Regime crackdowns test a movement's nonviolent discipline. For example, research finds that repression of recent civil resistance tactics increases a movement's risk of losing nonviolent discipline by up to 19 percent.[132]

Surprisingly, research also reveals that a movement's nonviolent discipline can begin to falter when a government makes concessions to the movement. Perhaps as a result of movement overconfidence, significant government concessions have been found to increase a movement's risk of losing nonviolent discipline by up to 40 percent.[133]

Both of these scenarios become more likely at times of peak mobilization. Since succumbing to violence against the regime abandons one of the movement's greatest advantages in the conflict, this risk merits significant attention.

First, activists and the public should be made aware of what the data reveals on this matter, and external actors can help in this process. Relative to violent insurgency, civil resistance has higher success rates, higher prospects of democratic consolidation, fosters far greater public participation, works more quickly, makes government repression more likely to backfire, is more likely to induce defections among an opponent's supporters, and is less likely to lead to atrocities or devolve to full-scale civil war.[134]

However, rather than transitioning to a full-fledged insurgency, another scenario in the face of repression is that a predominantly nonviolent movement develops a violent flank. This is an increasingly common phenomenon over the past decade. Between 1970 and 2009, approximately 30 percent to 35 percent of maximalist civil resistance movements had violent flanks, but that number increased to more than 50 percent between 2010 and 2019, during which time movement success rates also sharply declined.[135]

While violent flanks are on average less harmful to movements than full shifts to insurgency, they still create significant risks and downsides (including in the worst case of devolving into a violent insurgency). Movements with violent flanks suffer lower public participation rates, and an increase in both the likelihood and degree of state repression.[136] Movement violence and riots also can cut off possibilities for future growth, as sympathetic and neutral parties with potential to become allies instead develop negative views of the movement.[137] Riots also are found to be less likely to lead to government concessions than nonviolent resistance.[138]

For these reasons, external actors should consider taking actions that emphasize the importance of nonviolent discipline. Such actions can be an extension of work done in the early organizing phase. For example, strategic planning and development of a movement's DNA can emphasize the strategic advantages of remaining nonviolent. Past efforts to build unity and maximize participation should ensure significant engagement with women, whose organizations and frontline participation are associated with increased probability of maintaining nonviolent discipline. Movements that have a gender-inclusive ideology are also more likely to maintain nonviolent discipline.[139]

Ongoing public education campaigns (as outlined in the early organizing phase) may share relevant information about the comparative advantages of civil resistance and the risks of violence.

Validation and incentives also should be addressed. International media coverage is more likely when a movement develops a violent flank.[140] This creates an incentive for a movement to engage in violence, especially when it has repeatedly tried nonviolent means and been ignored. For this reason, public officials and others may want to proactively offer greater attention to nonviolent movements, even in early stages, and consistently validate their courageous and strategic choice of tactics. The belief that shifting to violence will attract international military support (as some argued in Syria in 2011 and ensuing years) must also be dispelled unambiguously.[141]

Thus, incentives need to flip: groups need to see that the support available to them when they are nonviolent can be cut off if they become violent. There is no perfect line in making this kind of determination—for example, as a movement becomes large, small groups outside of anyone's control may engage in opportunistic violence, or regimes may plant *agents provocateurs* at any stage of a movement to incite or engage in violence under the guise of the movement. But by relying on indicators such as a movement's core principles, statements from movement leaders, the content of movement trainings, and the practices of the vast majority of movement participants, a movement's nonviolent character can be discerned.

Ongoing Strategy Development

A further way external actors can support peak mobilization is through ongoing strategy development. During this phase, new events alter social, economic, and political dynamics regularly, and reveal new information about the conflict and the capabilities of each side.

Having a framework (i.e., relevant metrics identified in the early organizing phase) to evaluate new developments can help a movement quickly assimilate information and prioritize the most important factors when considering its options. Movements in peak mobilization may also need rapid responses to specific questions that emerge in their conflict (e.g., on topics as diverse as principles of effective labor strikes, financial relationships of regime elites, or guidance for effective collaboration between movements and political parties). Requests may also be made to amplify movement public communications, emphasize certain events in public statements, or for small amounts of funding.

In addition, as a movement's pressure begins to reveal previously latent cracks among a regime's allies (e.g., tensions among political and economic elites, or tensions within the police and military), inside information about the status of these groups becomes highly valuable in movement decision-making. External actors who have such knowledge may choose to share it with movements.

To meet this variety of needs, it is important to shift modalities from the early organizing phase. With time no longer an abundant resource, assistance during peak mobilization must become rapid in getting specific information and resources to movement activists, with few or no strings attached. Being prepared to conduct research based on movement needs, offering movements requested resources, and connecting movements with experts on various topics (from scholars and policymakers to activists in other countries who can share insights from their own experience) is important. In addition, sharing inside information about weaknesses and divisions within or among a regime's pillars of support can be highly valuable. Research shows that when a small- or moderate-sized movement targets its mobilization at wavering pillars of support, its probability of success increases.[142]

Fostering Defections

All regimes are comprised of groups and institutions that collectively generate power for regime leaders. These regime "pillars of support" include:

- State institutions including various branches of security forces, judiciary, and bureaucracy.

- Economic organizations such as corporate entities, the banking sector, and labor groups.

- Informational entities like state-allied media.

- Cultural and religious institutions.

• Other nongovernmental groups such as militias.

However, each pillar has its own interests and loyalties, and within each pillar, there are also differentials of interests and loyalties.

These latent fault lines both among and within pillars are normally hidden from the public, but civil resistance movements can create visible fractures. When these divisions lead to defections, it can be major factor in movement success: one study finds that a movement's success rate increases by nearly 60 percent when security force defections take place.[143] Movements also can proactively cultivate attributes and strategies that make defections more likely.[144]

External actors can further help to facilitate defections through a number of means. They can seek out channels for informal or formal communications between movement leadership and different factions serving under an authoritarian regime. They can gauge interests, positions, sentiment, and the potential of these factions to accommodate a movement's demands. Back channels between civil resistance leaders and regime insiders also can sometimes be opened to enable them to begin discussion of the terms of transition.

Countries that have significant formal and informal points of contact with foreign security services can try to establish communications between their own officers and counterparts abroad, advising these counterparts of the costs and risks of obeying an autocrat's orders to crack down on civil resisters (we discuss this in more detail in Pillar III, chapter 5).[145]

In addition, foreign states can lower the costs of defecting for regime elites, for example by offering protection to whistleblowers who speak up and leave the regime. To further reassure potential defectors, external actors can make pledges to economically and politically stabilize a nation in the post-transition phase, and offer to deploy human rights monitors during a transition to ensure that violent retribution does not take place against previous regime elites.[146]

PHASE 3: PROTRACTED STRUGGLE

The protracted struggle phase refers to a time in which peak mobilization has passed (as a result of repression or a movement's temporary exhaustion), but both the regime and the movement persist and continue to contend. While not all movements go through this phase (sometimes a single peak mobilization can achieve a movement's goals), many movements do experience protracted strug-

gle, which can last for years and may be punctuated by additional periods of peak mobilization.

During protracted struggle, disappointment can set in. Mobilizing involves elevating hopes, and long pent-up emotions can suddenly manifest with urgency. However, the average maximalist civil resistance movement lasts for three years, and movements that operate on the assumption that they must win within six weeks or six months tend to constrain their own strategic thinking.[147] Moreover, when high expectations based on an unrealistic time frame are not met, it can cause activists to become pessimistic, demobilize, or turn to violence out of frustration. It is ironic when a movement makes unprecedented progress in a short time and then concludes that it is losing, but this verdict by activists can quickly become a self-fulfilling prophecy. This is why metrics that were identified in the early organizing phase serve as important foundations for assessing past progress, and devising next steps.

Challenges and opportunities in the protected struggle phase involve sustaining movement engagement over longer periods of time, continuing to build movement strength (i.e., ongoing training efforts, and coalition building) and offensive capacities against the regime, continuing to refine its strategic and transition planning, and building structures within movements that can help it endure.

In particular, the protracted struggle phase is a time when movements may invest more in developing alternative institutions: i.e., media, governance structures, transition planning committees, neighborhood committees, educational entities, training capacities, conflict resolution bodies, and alternative economic structures. For example, after the Polish Solidarity movement's peak mobilization in 1980-81 was met with repression, Solidarity went underground and developed its own media and communications capacities (samizdat) and alternative educational structures, among others, to help sustain the movement, which reemerged and won a negotiated democratic transition in 1989.

External actors can help movements during protracted struggle, but first they must also resist erroneous conclusions that a movement has lost simply because it has not achieved full victory in a short period of time, or because mobilization and media attention has (possibly temporarily) declined.

To provide support, external actors can draw from repertoires used in both the early organizing phase (i.e., strategic planning support to help a movement regroup) as well as the peak mobilization phase (i.e., building international pressure on the regime, raising the cost of repres-

Former Belarusian paratroopers take part in a protest against the presidential election results and demand the resignation of Belarusian President Alexander Lukashenko and the release of political prisoners, near the Government House in Independence Square in Minsk, Belarus August 16, 2020. REUTERS/Vasily Fedosenko

sion, mitigating repression's impact, and fostering defections). They also can use a period of protracted struggle to increase coordination with other external actors. If activists request it, external actors may further offer to help mediate directly between the movement and the regime.

PHASE 4: TRANSITION

The transition phase occurs when there is a formalized process to accommodate movement demands. In some cases, this takes place during a short phase of negotiation, lasting days or weeks. In others, such as an election, there are aspects of negotiation (i.e., throughout a political campaign, assembling a winning coalition, and making personnel appointments upon victory), and there may also be an interregnum between the election and a candidate assuming office. However, notably, not all movements experience a transition phase, since some transition mechanisms—i.e., a resignation of a leader, or a coup d'état—happen suddenly with little formal process or warning.

The particular mechanism by which a transition happens— negotiation, election, resignation, external intervention,

coup d'état, or regime collapse—has substantial implications for democracy.[148] Negotiated and electoral transitions tend to result in more democratic outcomes, which is attributed to the fact that these two mechanisms tend to institutionalize new arrangements, rebalance power, and allow movement actors to remain more fully in the driver seat of the transition. Resignations can share some of these characteristics, and external interventions, coups, and regime collapses appear to have the lowest probability of major democratic gains or consolidation, although there can be exceptions.[149]

External actors will therefore want to encourage movements to seek negotiated or electoral transitions when possible. This can mean preparing movements for the fact that these mechanisms can entail compromise (i.e., an electoral candidate may not align perfectly with a movement's positions) and/or a willingness to negotiate directly with elements of a regime (which requires one or more individuals to represent the movement and its positions).

External actors also can support negotiations in a number of ways. They can set up brain trusts, sometimes with help from diaspora populations, to provide ideas and contextual or specialized knowledge relevant to democratic political transitions (i.e., legal matters and transitional justice processes). In addition, they can make pledges of future economic support and security, which can assure fence-sitters that any transition will be orderly with prospects of economic growth and stability. Lastly, external actors can discourage coups and warn of their consequences.

To help consolidate gains during the transition period, new commitments should be accompanied by the establishment of new institutions, norms, procedures, and personnel appointments that put movement supporters in positions of formal influence.[150] These arrangements help to lock in progress that has been made. In addition, any reserve domains of unaccountable power demanded by former regime elites should be viewed with suspicion. For example, lack of civilian control of security forces after political transitions in Sudan and Myanmar helped to unravel subsequent democratic gains over ensuing years. Rejecting such positions and returning to active civil resistance in some cases may be a preferable course of action than agreeing with these demands.

PHASE 5: POST-TRANSITION

The post-transition phase occurs when a movement has achieved its primary goal and must consolidate and protect its gains. During this phase, the movement's unity risks fragmenting, demobilization becomes more likely, and a movement's opponents often start quietly to plot a comeback. Challenges and opportunities involve holding the government to its new commitments, maintaining popular pressure on institutions to uphold the rule of law, advocating for accountability for past perpetrators of abuse, and remaining vigilant about attempts at an authoritarian comeback.

Evidence from Sudan, Egypt, Tunisia, Serbia, Georgia, Ukraine, and other countries shows that authoritarian leaders and parties do not stop contending for power after a civil resistance-driven transition has occurred. In fact, in some cases such parties may reunify themselves in the face of what they view as a newly threatening democratic status quo. This compounds numerous other challenges in post-transition contexts, as stated earlier in this playbook, including addressing corruption; inequitable concentration of power; questions of justice and impunity; and the need to modify, discard, or redevelop various institutions and laws. Security challenges and societal polarization may also need to be addressed, and meanwhile the government must continue to deliver services and economic performance.

These well-documented circumstances are the focus of many existing forms of democracy support, which should continue for a long period until democratic "rules of the game" are clearly established. Civil society advocates and independent media must become well rooted, and previously authoritarian parties and leaders must be largely abandoned in favor of leaders and parties that show loyalty to democratic process and results. To achieve these outcomes, however, often requires additional episodes of civil resistance, which means that it is important that a movement not disband entirely, or lose all its leadership to political parties.

For example, long-term transition processes (i.e., drafting a new constitution) that exclude meaningful citizen input may become the target of civil resistance, as excluded groups seek to make their voices heard. Civil resistance may at times be necessary to hold new (or old) elites accountable, address long-standing systemic problems of corruption, and ensure that new political arrangements reflect the aspirations of the movement that drove the transition. While such disruptions may seem to threaten short-term stability, they can also prevent the adoption of institutional arrangements that could lead to far greater disruption in the future.

Thus, new governments favored by external actors will likely have to endure civil resistance challenges when their leaders and institutions fail to live up to their democratic obligations. Rather than seeing this as unwelcome development, external actors should recognize that this is often an essential aspect of addressing corruption and creating accountable government. They should be ready to play a watchdog role when new governments confront their own mobilized nonviolent citizenry.[151]

However, civil resistance during the post-transition phase can also harm democracy, if it is used to contest legitimate democratic outcomes or advance narrow partisan interests, and movements must avoid this trap. For example, if institutions are functioning properly, an election campaign should primarily consist of electioneering—not civil resistance. Unless there is evidence of malfeasance, civil resistance should also not be part of a repertoire to contest the results. After the election, civil resistance can be used to hold the winners to account if they abuse their positions, and to support rule of law and institutional checks and balances of democratic government.[152]

Pillar I: Policy Recommendations

Recommendation #1: Elevate democracy as a key national interest.

- **The US government should elevate supporting democracy to be a central factor in foreign policy decision-making.** The president should direct the national security agencies and the national security advisor to weigh implications for democracy in all major foreign policy decisions. In addition, the president should issue a National Security Strategy or directive for supporting democracy overseas. Such a directive would send a strong signal to US allies, and authoritarian regimes, that the United States is committed to supporting democracy overseas.

- **The European Union and other democratic governments should implement similar measures** to ensure that supporting democracy and combatting authoritarianism are reflected as key national interests.

Recommendation #2: Invest in new options and coordination to support and foster the capacities of pro-democracy civil resistance movements.

- **Departments and agencies within the US government should set up working groups to review options and establish improved processes for supporting movements, and a US government-wide working group should be established to help coordinate support.** Establishing this government-wide "home" from which movement support can be coordinated, as well as working groups within individual departments and agencies, will facilitate increased collaboration on roles and responsibilities (i.e., securing visas, offering funding, developing sanctions), and thus more effective support.

- **The US Congress should establish a fund to support innovative programs aimed at reversing authoritarianism and providing assistance to civil resistance movements.** A pillar of this fund should focus on building core infrastructure to support movements (i.e., educational and skill-building initiatives, efforts to promote unity among opposition groups), and resourcing cutting-edge programs to revitalize stalled—or cement gains of surging—democratic movements. Congress should mandate to the executive branch that innovation—and risk taking—are requirements. To win the conflict with authoritarians and their enablers, new resources will be essential.

- **With the White House leading, executive branch agencies that are the primary funders of democracy assistance**—the US Agency for International Development (USAID) and the Department of State—**need to be more forward leaning on support to civil resistance movements.** This will entail USAID and State eliciting and welcoming novel programmatic approaches, many not tried before, for supporting movements, as well as understanding—and accepting—that there will be some failure. Funding should provide flexibility to the implementer to pivot among targets and adjust spending, based on movement needs, and allow multiyear awards, which will allow partners and movements to conduct medium- to long-term planning.

- Democratic governments should **increase the quantity and amount of multiyear funding to increase movement training and skill building**, providing such funds to nongovernmental organizations. Allies should prioritize support for rapid small grants for equipment, transport, convening space, and other short-term movement needs.

- Democratic governments should **support establishment of international strike funds** through, i.e., through grants to international nongovernmental organizations, and increase resources available for urgent/emergency assistance to activists under threat, through new or existing capabilities like the lifeline assistance fund or other USAID-rapid response capacities.

- Democratic governments should **use their convening power** to bring together international nongovernmental organizations (advocacy and philanthropy), CSOs, diaspora groups, and movement activists (if possible, given the local context and security situation) during nascent movement stages to discuss coordination of external support.

- Democratic governments should **support activists gathering and engaging in dialogue**, crafting a common vision for the future of their country, and planning and developing unity on elements of democratic transition plans. Brain trusts may also be developed to advise on transition processes (i.e., legislative or constitutional changes, transitional justice processes) or other phases of a movement's growth.

- Democratic governments should **expand the quantity of multiyear funding available to support the growth of educational infrastructure** for activists internationally through international nongovernmental organizations. More is needed to resource new research and the development of new educational resources in civil resistance, which can be made freely available, in English and other languages. Useful research can be academic or applied, and focus on topics that activists or external actors have predefined as being relevant to their work. New educational resources would take generic civil resistance insights and localize them to particular regions, focusing on particular regional issues (i.e., countering corruption), drawing on relevant regional examples, and being available in relevant regional languages.

- Democratic governments should **dedicate resources to support initiatives aimed at advancing an enabling legal environment for human rights movements**. Such initiatives should include: a) advocacy to reform laws that are used to chill and punish nonviolent collective action, and advocacy to promote enabling legislation; b) tools and activities to help activists and movements navigate restrictive legal environments; and c) emergency legal and financial assistance and other vital protection for movement members who are targeted.

Recommendation #3: Augment and reposition diplomatic services to enhance movement support.

- Democratic governments should **organize their embassies to enhance outreach to movements**. Embassies in key countries should dedicate at least one political officer to proactively broaden their contacts to engage with movement actors as well as regularly monitor and analyze movement developments. This will involve an expansive concept of civil society, and include reaching out to groups and associations that may be small, community-based, unregistered, and/or outside of major cities. This political officer should work to develop options for movement support and communicate with allied embassies to coordinate support. Governments can dedicate additional communications staff in embassies in key countries when movement activity is anticipated or ongoing.

- Democratic governments should **provide increased diplomatic training on civil resistance movements and transitions**. The US Foreign Service Institute, USAID University, and similar training institutes in other democracies should add modules on civil resistance and democratic transitions (i.e., how civil resistance works, principles of external support) and make these courses a mandatory part of foreign service officer training. Professional development seminars should also be proactively held in missions abroad. The US State Department and other foreign ministries should provide greater professional incentives (career advancement, promotions, awards, and public recognition) for foreign service officers to specialize in human rights work and directly engage with civil society.

Recommendation #4: Support independent media internationally and locally.

- Democratic governments should **significantly increase funding and technical assistance to create infrastructures of support for independent media.** Such support may aim to increase independent international news coverage, local news outlets, and movement-based media outlets. The presence of these forms of media are associated with positive impacts for civil resistance movements. Funding and technical assistance could help with start-up costs, the development of effective business models, internal governance and accountability structures, investigative journalism, journalist training and education, the establishment of professional associations, and efforts to protect journalists and media outlets under threat.

- Democratic governments should **coordinate to vigorously push back against attempts to intimidate, silence, or restrict free press.** Attacks on free press should be seen as a leading indicator of democratic backsliding, and trigger swift multilateral responses.

4. Pillar II: Developing a New Normative Framework—the Right to Assistance (R2A)

Collective actions by democratic governments, willing multilateral institutions, and international nongovernmental organizations (including advocacy and philanthropy) are all necessary to reverse the authoritarian tide. Developing a shared normative framework for movement support—a broadly recognized right to assistance (R2A)—could go a long way toward legitimizing support for nonviolent civil resistance movements and enable greater international participation and collaboration in such efforts.

The concept behind R2A is straightforward: regardless of where they live, people have the right to request and receive assistance in order to protect and advance fundamental human rights.

Advancing this normative framework would directly challenge autocratic governments that have asserted, with increasing success over the last two decades, their own de facto norm of "hyper-sovereignty." Based on this norm, they grant themselves carte blanche to engage in domestic repression, curtail international efforts to support democracy, and brazenly block accountability for themselves and their allies in the UN and other fora. Meanwhile, they also betray their own arguments by aggressively attacking and undermining democratic states.

This status quo cannot stand: the unspoken end point of authoritarian claims is that they can act with impunity while international human rights are reduced to a dead letter. This has ramifications for democracy everywhere, but thus far democratic pushback has been tepid. Scholar Tom Ginsburg writes:

International law is becoming both a shield and a sword, insulating authoritarians from criticism while also increasingly allowing them to affect developments beyond their borders. Democracies ought to be vigilant, and must contest these norms on the international plane or risk steepening the slope of democratic decline . . .

To confront authoritarian international law, there is no substitute for active engagement by democracies, as democracies.[153]

Rising to this competition, the right to assistance would be grounded in international law, but would not depend on the UN for formal invocation.[154] Rather, it would be developed and embraced by a group of democracies (such as the G7; a new D-10; or a broader new coalition or alliance of democracies), and its initial formulation would have three goals:[155]

- Establish baseline forms of assistance that can be requested by populations in countries throughout the world.

- Contextualize acts of civil resistance within international human rights law.

- Justify additional options for support when governments repress populations that are exercising their human rights.

Ultimately, R2A will only be as strong as the unity of those who stand behind it, and their willingness to take action accordingly. Democracies can start to build consensus among themselves by articulating the specific parameters to which they agree regarding these three goals. Below, we offer points to inform further discussions.

1. **The right to assistance is an extension of existing, internationally recognized human rights.**

   The foundation of R2A is that it is legitimate for people to request and receive various forms of support, subject to certain limitations. On this issue, numerous relevant international and regional treaties, UN General Assembly resolutions, and statements and practices of other international institutions (such as the Human Rights Committee and other treaty-established entities) provide support for such a right.[156]

   In particular, R2A emerges from the right to freedom of association, which is recognized in a range of international declarations and legal instruments, including the Universal Declaration of Human Rights (article 20), the International Covenant on Civil and Political Rights (article 22), the Convention on the Elimination of All Forms of Discrimination against Women (article 7), the Declaration on Human Rights Defenders (article 5), as well as several regional conventions covering Africa, Europe, the Americas, and the Middle East.[157]

One of the most widely recognized treaties addressing this topic, article 22, part 1, of the International Covenant on Civil and Political Rights (ICCPR), reads:

1. Everyone shall have the right to freedom of association with others, including the right to form and join trade unions for the protection of his interests.[158]

Freedom of association includes the right to request, receive, and use resources.[159] As Maina Kiai, former UN special rapporteur on the rights to freedom of peaceful assembly and of association, states:

*The ability to seek, secure, and use resources is essential to the existence and effective operations of any association, no matter how small. The right to freedom of association not only includes the ability of individuals or legal entities to form and join an association but also to **seek, receive and use resources**—human, material and financial—from domestic, foreign, and international sources.[160] (emphasis added)*

Kiai elaborates that these resources are quite broad, including:

Financial transfers (e.g., donations, grants, contracts, sponsorships, social investments, etc.); loan guarantees and other forms of financial assistance from natural and legal persons; in-kind donations (e.g., contributions of goods, services, software and other forms of intellectual property, real property, etc.); material resources (e.g., office supplies, IT equipment, etc.); human resources (e.g., paid staff, volunteers, etc.); access to international assistance, solidarity; ability to travel and communicate without undue interference and the right to benefit from the protection of the State.[161]

Examples of additional support from treaty law and UN declarations for the right to assistance include:[162]

- Article 6 of the Declaration on the Elimination of All Forms of Intolerance and of Discrimination Based on Religion or Belief, stating that: "The right to freedom of thought, conscience, religion or belief shall include...[freedom to] solicit and receive voluntary financial and other contributions from individuals and institutions."[163]

- Human Rights Committee communication 1274/2004, stating that "the Committee observes that the right to freedom of association relates not only to the right to form an association, but also

guarantees the right of such an association freely to carry out its statutory activities. The protection afforded by [ICCPR] article 22 extends to all activities of an association."[164]

- Human Rights Council resolution 22/6, which calls on states: "To ensure that reporting requirements placed on individuals, groups and organs of society do not inhibit functional autonomy"; "To ensure that they do not discriminatorily impose restrictions on potential sources of funding. . . "; and to ensure "that no law should criminalize or delegitimize activities in defence of human rights on account of the origin of funding thereto."[165]

- Article 13 of the Declaration on Human Rights Defenders states that: "Everyone has the right, individually and in association with others, to solicit, receive and utilize resources for the express purpose of promoting and protecting human rights and fundamental freedoms through peaceful means, in accordance with article 3 of the present Declaration."[166]

However, the right to freedom of association, and thus the right to assistance, is not without limit. Article 22, part 2, of the ICCPR reads:

No restrictions may be placed on the exercise of this right other than those which are prescribed by law and which are necessary in a democratic society in the interests of national security or public safety, public order (ordre public), the protection of public health or morals or the protection of the rights and freedoms of others. This article shall not prevent the imposition of lawful restrictions on members of the armed forces and of the police in their exercise of this right.[167]

Thus, there are three conditions that restrictions must meet in order to be lawful: they must intend to address one of the identified interests above; have a basis in law; and be "necessary in a democratic society."[168]

In practice, this means that restrictions must be proportionate and narrow. For example, using the pretext of public health or public safety to arbitrarily and indiscriminately curtail any association's right to request and receive assistance would be unlawful. Restrictions would instead have to be tailored narrowly to meet the legitimate state interest.[169] It also means that the government has a burden of proof before restrictions can be enacted. For example, curtailing resources to an organization (i.e., an organization that happens to be

Protestors take to the streets after Russian President Vladimir Putin authorized a military operation in eastern Ukraine, in Saint Petersburg, Russia, February 24, 2022. The placard reads: 'No to war!' REUTERS/Anton Vaganov

critical of the government) based on unsubstantiated accusations of illegal activity is also unlawful.

Claiming protection of state sovereignty is also, by itself, insufficient justification to curtail the right to freedom of association. Such a claim has been made by many authoritarians with the intent to arbitrarily restrict and pressure civil society organizations engaged in human rights, anti-corruption efforts, and pro-democracy activities. Yet as then-Special Rapporteur Kiai notes:

The protection of State sovereignty is not listed as a legitimate interest in the [ICCPR]....States cannot refer to additional grounds, even those provided by domestic legislation, and cannot loosely interpret international obligations to restrict the right to freedom of association....Affirming that national security is threatened when an association receives funding from [a] foreign source is not only spurious and distorted, but also in contradiction with international human rights law.

Associations, whether domestic- or foreign-funded, should therefore be free to promote their views—even minority and dissenting views, [and] challenge governments about their human rights record or campaign for democratic reforms, with-

out being accused of treason and other defamatory terms. (emphasis added)[170]

Nonetheless, the three identified conditions for restricting freedom of association allow for reasonable limits. For example, in furtherance of the interest of national security, a government could require transparency on international support received and prohibit receipt of resources by government officials or electoral candidates.

In these and other cases, however, the time, place and manner of restriction matters. Simple notification and validation procedures of funds received are generally legitimate. On the other hand, "transparency" laws that require that all NGO-bound funds pass through a government intermediary violate the recipient's rights. Allowing NGOs to receive such funds but then requiring them to request government permission for any use of such funds would also be a violation.[171] Creating foreign labeling requirements that are then turned into a basis for the government to publicly incite threats against a nongovernmental organization would also be a violation.

2. Acts of civil resistance are protected under international human rights law.

The articulation of a right to assistance is likely to be met by authoritarian regimes claiming that their ability to restrict civil society is based on "sound" national security grounds. Authoritarians label civil resistance as foreign-backed regime change in an attempt to justify their crackdowns and marginalize human rights concerns. They characterize popular nonviolent movements demanding democracy as a foreign act of war, a criminal conspiracy, or a terrorist threat.[172]

Unsurprisingly, these conspiratorial claims are not grounded in fact. Civil resistance movements are driven by widespread, voluntary mobilization by people in a society seeking to redress their grievances and/or achieve their aspirations. Moreover, many acts of civil resistance involve the exercise of legally protected human rights. Mass demonstrations, boycotts, labor strikes and numerous other nonviolent actions enact human rights enshrined in various treaties, including:

- The International Covenant on Civil and Political Rights (ICCPR)

- African Charter on Human and Peoples' Rights

- The European Convention on Human Rights and Fundamental Freedoms (ECHR)

- The American Convention on Human Rights

- The Convention on the Elimination of All Forms of Racial Discrimination

Specifically, legal scholar Elizabeth A. Wilson examines the rights involved in nonviolent protest and concludes that protest "implicates political participation rights; the rights to opinion, information, and expression; and rights of peaceful assembly and association."[173] She also reinforces the idea of a right to assistance, by commenting that in order to be fully effectuated, some human rights are conjoined with secondary rights:

It has been suggested that the right to [nonviolent] protest is "a supporting or instrumental freedom that [goes] together with and facilitate[s] the realization of other rights and freedoms."[174] Some of these primary rights...[correspond] to the secondary right to provide support to nonviolent actors. The right to receive information...[corresponds] to the right to impart information. The right to associate with those willing to provide support...[corresponds to] the right to associate with those who wish to receive support.[175]

Thus, many nonviolent tactics used by pro-democracy movements are protected by international human rights law. That said, the time, place, and manner of an act of civil resistance can influence how it is regarded, and in extreme cases, this can allow the state to restrict the exercise of these rights. For example, article 21 of the International Covenant on Civil and Political Rights allows for restrictions on the right of peaceful assembly that are:

Imposed in conformity with the law and which are necessary in a democratic society in the interests of national security or public safety, public order (ordre public), the protection of public health or morals or the protection of the rights and freedoms of others.[176]

By this standard, a nonviolent blockade cutting off access to a hospital and which results in injury and death of patients can be treated differently than a blockade of a road with no such effects. Violence by protesters would also put them in a different category than nonviolent demonstrations. However, if only some participants at a protest engage in violence, the state must be discriminate in its response—it cannot treat all protesters present as "violent" based on violent acts by only some.[177]

3. A government's sovereignty and the norm of nonintervention are not absolute.

The common counterargument to any form of international assistance to movements is that sovereignty and the norm of nonintervention allow a head of state to curtail external support that it finds undesirable.

However, this argument is not as compelling as it might appear. The norm of nonintervention was first conceived of as an embargo against armed intervention in other countries—it is less clear the extent to which it may embargo other forms of cross-border support, particularly the transfer of information.[178]

Furthermore, the concept of state sovereignty itself can be construed as inherently residing in the population of a country, as opposed to its head of state. Thus a head of state can assert sovereignty only to the extent that its population has opportunities to regularly and freely express its preference to vest its sovereignty in a particular government. In the case of rulers who stifle democracy and accountability, they are hardly in the position to claim that they represent their countries' populations, and therefore their assertions of sovereignty are faulty.[179]

Moreover, there are rights of self-determination and political participation that cannot be erased by the edicts of self-proclaimed sovereigns. For example, article 1 of the International Covenant on Civil and Political Rights states that:[180]

All peoples have the right to self-determination. By virtue of that right they freely determine their political status and freely pursue their economic, social, and cultural development.[181]

Article 25 states that:

Every citizen shall have the right and the opportunity....:

(a) To take part in the conduct of public affairs, directly or through freely chosen representatives;

(b) To vote and to be elected at genuine periodic elections which shall be by universal and equal suffrage and shall be held by secret ballot, guaranteeing the free expression of the will of the electors;

(c) To have access, on general terms of equality, to public service in his country.[182]

If these recognized human rights are to have meaning in the real world, they can be cited to argue against arbitrary claims of authoritarian sovereignty.[183] As scholar Michael Ignatieff states:

The legitimacy of collective self-determination—the right of states to be sovereign—derives in turn from individual self-determination, the right of individuals to be free. If this individual right is crushed, an individual retains the right to appeal for help outside, and those outside have a duty to assist.[184]

Implications for Establishing a Right to Assistance

The aforementioned points have several implications for establishing a right to assistance.

First, pro-democracy civil resistance movements are the result of thousands or millions of citizens exercising their universally recognized human rights, which the authoritarian seeks to deny. This means democracies must stand firm in the face of false authoritarian assertions that movements are a form of foreign-backed regime change, or a violent threat. The burden of proof for such spurious charges rests on authoritarians, not on the democracies that stand with these movements. Authoritarian governments do not have a legal basis to contravene the human rights of their citizens.

Second, assertions that civil resistance movements are foreign controlled are not based in fact. Instead, these movements are driven by indigenous energy and widespread voluntary mobilization. There is no foreign power that can compel thousands or millions of people to join and sustain their involvement in a nonviolent movement, often incurring personal risk in the process. External actors may try to support these movements, but this does not mean that movements are controlled by the external actors, nor that movements depend on them.

Third, authoritarian claims of sovereignty and assertions of non-interference are not adequate grounds to curtail a right to assistance.

Fourth, as an opening step to advance R2A, a group of democracies could come to agreement about clear minimum standards about how they respect their populations' right to assistance, and then call on other states—many of whom are signatories to international human rights treaties—to equally respect their population's human rights by meeting these standards. As part of this process, they could also develop criteria for movements to request and receive assistance, which could include that a movement is nonviolent, and that the movement's goals are consistent with democracy and internationally recognized human rights.

This approach would have several benefits including:

- The norm would be agnostic of regime type. It would not require labeling regimes as either "democratic," "authoritarian," or "backsliding" to determine the standards to which they are held. Rather the norm would be relevant to all.

- Even with a relatively conservative definition of R2A, a great deal of impactful support to movements would be permitted. For example, information exchange and modest amounts of funding for convenings and workshops can have a major impact, if timed well and adapted to local needs.

- The norm would be a countervailing influence in backsliding democracies. One of the challenging aspects of backsliding is that it often involves an accumulation of technical changes that weaken democracy, but these technical changes are regarded as being within a state's sovereign purview. For example, tweaks to voter registration requirements, shifts in democratic norms, modified vetting procedures for new judges, or changes to permitting procedures for media outlets, are generally not matters on which foreign intervention is seen as legitimate. However, when aspiring autocrats begin to

Members of Sudan's alliance of opposition and protest groups chant slogans outside Sudan's Central Bank during the second day of a strike, as tensions mounted with the country's military rulers over the transition to democracy, in Khartoum, Sudan May 29, 2019. REUTERS/Mohamed Nureldin Abdallah

curtail civil society's rights, they move into a domain in which their governments have clearer international human rights obligations. Thus, developing a norm based on international human rights standards provides a basis for earlier pressure on backsliding democracies, without violating their sovereignty. Moreover, the right to assistance would enable support to be received by those (in civil society) who are often best positioned to contest the many incremental domestic cuts that characterize backsliding.

• The norm enables proportional responses to transgressions. For example, if an authoritarian requires transparency of assistance and then uses that as a basis for surveillance and generating arrest lists, recipients of support and external actors would no longer be bound to comply with the transparency requirement. Since the authoritarian's use of the requirement is not "necessary in a democratic society," it would be a breach of their state's human rights obligations. In the face of such a breach, a proportional response by other parties is a legitimate remedy.

Subsequent steps to establishing the norm could include developing criteria for civil resistance movements to receive formal legal recognition, and potentially the establishment of technical oversight bodies for R2A. Already, movements are implicitly recognized in international law in some cases (i.e., in African Union decisions about government recognition), and making such recognition explicit may incentivize populations to choose nonviolent strategies of change.[185]

In addition, if civil resistance movements become legally recognized under international law, this could potentially be a step toward developing international frameworks to regulate their conflicts with regimes. This has been done before with violent conflict—it may be possible to do so as well with civil resistance.[186]

Pillar II: Policy Recommendations

Recommendation #5: Establish a multilateral task force to develop R2A.

- **Democratic governments should establish a multilateral task force to assess the feasibility of advancing an internationally recognized right to assistance**, potentially under the auspices of the G7 or another entity comprised of leading democracies.

- Democratic governments should **launch formal multistakeholder dialogues on the potential design, adoption, and implementation of a right to assistance**, involving and seeking input and comment from governments, international nongovernmental organizations (advocacy and philanthropy), CSOs, diaspora groups, and activists. The principals administering these dialogues should be adequately resourced so as to be able to proactively reach out to groups, substantively interact with them, and seek their comments; and be able to allocate research funds when needed to support the development of international legal, strategic, or other aspects of designing, adopting, and implementing a right to assistance.

Recommendation #6: Renew commitment to key international human rights laws and norms.

- Democratic governments should **renew and expand their efforts to defend international human rights law and norms**, in particular those relating to the freedoms of association, assembly, and expression. Moreover, such governments must actively defend civil resistance and provide support to it, as consistent with internationally recognized and protected human rights.

- Democratic governments should **increase their engagement with multilateral organizations that create and uphold international human rights norms** and provide mechanisms to raise the diplomatic and reputational costs when those norms are violated by authoritarian states.

5. Pillar III: Strengthening Democratic Solidarity to Pressure and Constrain Repressive Regimes

As democratic states develop better methods to enable and support movements, they must also increase their solidarity and efforts to pressure authoritarian regimes. These activities are interrelated because imposing costs on autocrats means that autocrats will respond in kind. Thus, greater democratic unity and strength enables greater democratic offense.

To achieve this, we first discuss possibilities for new alliances to increase coordination and resilience. Then we address several efforts that democracies can take to constrain authoritarians. Lastly, we outline a framework of escalatory responses for when autocrats engage in repression against movements demanding democracy and human rights.

Building Democratic Solidarity

Democracies stand a better chance of pressuring autocrats if they can align policies and actions. The G7 provides an existing platform for influential democracies to act, and its members constitute over fifty percent of global gross domestic product.[187] However, the G7 is limited to major transatlantic democracies plus Japan, and in the face of common threats, there are opportunities to form wider coalitions.

One option is the establishment of an informal working group that consists of leading democracies. Alternatively, the United States and its allies could establish a new standing body, such as a D-10 or a broader coalition of democracies with a mandate to develop strategy and coordinate execution of joint democracy support and counterauthoritarian efforts.[188] The informal working group, or new standing body, would engage perspectives from every major region to identify threats and develop solutions to address them.

Whatever its form, an alliance of influential democracies could impose costs on autocratic regimes, incentivize their behavior change, and develop mechanisms to provide assistance to targeted democracies. As a core function, it could use its economic influence to defend against external attacks. For example, if one or more members of the alliance was subject to economic coercion by an authoritarian state (as China in the past has attempted against Australia and Lithuania), a mutual defense provision could be activated that would trigger economic support to the targeted state(s). This "Economic Article V" (to draw an analogy from NATO) could serve as a significant deterrent to authoritarian efforts to bully democracies, and enable greater resilience as democracies go on offense.[189]

The alliance could also help invigorate support for pro-democracy movements around the world by advancing the norm of a right to assistance, and adopt coordinated approaches and tools to support civil resistance movements through all phases of development. More broadly, it could orchestrate impactful public engagement efforts to highlight the dangers of authoritarianism, and the instrumental value and tangible benefits of democracy, aimed at influencing audiences around the world.[190]

Raising the Cost of Autocratic Repression and Subversion

A democratic alliance, or any grouping of democracies, can take coordinated actions to constrain and impose costs on authoritarian regimes. These actions may include heightening visibility of regime and movement actions, withdrawing support from autocracies, coordinating sanctions, increasing judicial accountability, leveraging military contact for democratic persuasion, and expanding efforts to disrupt authoritarian influence operations. A number of these actions are relatively low-resource options with high-impact potential, and could be taken on an ongoing basis. We outline them below.

HEIGHTENING VISIBILITY OF REGIME AND MOVEMENT ACTIONS

External actors can monitor developments, draw attention to regime abuses, and condemn them through multiple channels. They also can elevate voices from a movement and highlight examples of courageous and strategic civil resistance. For example, visiting dignitaries can assign the same priority to meetings with civil society groups as they do with foreign government officials.[191] Diplomats may engage in coordinated actions with their counterparts from other democratic states to show collective presence and support for human rights and democracy. They can further attend activist trials and observe public movement activities, thereby serving as monitors and an indirect protective presence.

The results of these and other actions will depend significantly on context, which is why soliciting and responding to movement requests for assistance, and seeking movement consent before taking action, is critical. For example, quantitative research on condemnations by foreign governments and international organizations have found them, on average, to "have very little effect on [civil resistance movement] success."[192] However, that does not mean that in some cases condemnations have beneficial effects, such as when the United States condemns abuses through multiple channels in countries whose governments it has previously supported, or who depend on US aid, trade, or security assistance. Likewise, sometimes condemnations from nongovernmental actors, historically including Pope John Paul II, or transnational solidarity networks, can have mobilizing impacts domestically or abroad.[193]

To further monitor and heighten visibility, governments also can take actions that support independent media in an effort to make any regime repression backfire.[194] A study published in the *Journal of Peace Research* finds that movements that develop their own "parallel media institutions" are five times more likely to produce domestic backfire (via heightened movement mobilization and/or regime defections) than movements without, and thirteen times more likely to produce international backfire (via sanctions).[195] Likewise significant international media coverage of a movement increases the likelihood that repression will backfire internationally, particularly in the form of withdrawal of foreign government support.[196]

WITHDRAWING SUPPORT

Research finds that withdrawal of state support from autocrats can be "pivotal" to the success of civil resistance movements.[197] This is logical, since it signals an autocrat's declining international support, challenges the legitimacy of the government's recent actions, denies it practical material or other assistance, and can cause people within a regime's domestic pillars of support to question the regime's sustainability. Examples of this include France's withdrawal of support for the Ben Ali government in Tunisia, and the United States' ultimate withdrawals of support from the Mubarak regime in Egypt, the Pinochet regime in Chile, and the Marcos regime in the Philippines.

Assessing the impact of such actions, Chenoweth examined what forms of backfire against repression are the most potent, and identifies withdrawal of foreign support—along with heightened domestic mobilization and defections by regime elites and security forces—as having the most powerful impact:

> *Even without the withdrawal of support from a regime ally or domestic defections, the chances of success for a nonviolent campaign increase by over 20 percent from the smallest to the largest campaigns. But critically, once a regime ally does withdraw support, the chances for success among the largest campaigns double to over 40 percent. Add domestic security force loyalty shifts and elite defections, and the chance of success rockets up to about 45 percent for the smallest campaigns and 85 percent for the largest campaigns.[198]*

COORDINATING SANCTIONS

Economic sanctions can be either broad (affecting an entire country) or targeted (focused on specific entities or individuals). Evidence shows that the threat of either kind of sanctions can stimulate protest activity against regimes, especially when such threats are made by multiple governments.[199]

However, once imposed, sanctions no longer seem to have this stimulative effect on protest, and their impact

Britain's Prime Minister Boris Johnson, Japan's Prime Minister Fumio Kishida, U.S. President Joe Biden, Germany's Chancellor Olaf Scholz, European Commission President Ursula von der Leyen, France's President Emmanuel Macron, Canadian Prime Minister Justin Trudeau and Italy's Prime Minister Mario Draghi attend a meeting alongside the G7 leaders summit at Bavaria's Schloss Elmau, near Garmisch-Partenkirchen, Germany June 28, 2022. Stefan Rousseau/Pool via REUTERS

varies depending on context and the type of sanction imposed. For this reason, it is incumbent upon external actors to engage with movements and seek their views on advisability, design, and possible repercussions before determining whether and how to proceed.[200]

Broad sanctions have proven a powerful tool, but they carry significant risks for movements and a country's civilian population. They are often credited with effective pressure on the apartheid government in South Africa (notably, the sanctions were requested by movement supporters). In addition, broad sanctions can also degrade an authoritarian regime's capacity to wage armed conflict, which could in some cases have beneficial effects for local movements.

However, it appears that these sanctions often provide advantages to autocrats who wish to repress movements.[201] Economic hardship can divert a population's energies that might otherwise be applied to civil resistance, and they enable autocrats to attribute such hardship to external actors rather than the failings of their regime.[202] At their worst, these sanctions can contribute to humanitarian crises.

In addition, broad sanctions can make it more challenging for external actors to support activists on the ground, as has happened in Iran, Sudan, and Syria.[203] Requiring non-governmental organizations to seek special authorization to provide assistance to civil society groups, and trying to comply with sanctions laws, can divert critical resources away from support activities, or simply become an insurmountable barrier to further engagement.

In contrast, targeted sanctions (also called "smart" sanctions) are narrow, seeking to impose costs and accountability on particular perpetrators or enablers of abuse, and they can be used on individuals or entities within even allied states. Their specific impacts on movements are understudied, but generally speaking, their tailored focus is more likely to minimize externalities on a country's population.

Smart sanctions are more powerful when they are implemented multilaterally, which requires coordination, and a new democratic alliance could help achieve this. Their effective use starts with identifying the individuals and entities that should be targeted, often through research, intelligence gathering, and civil society input. In addition, once sanctions are imposed, targets seek to evade them and find alternative means of gaining resources, and this requires regular and ongoing efforts to map evolving illicit relationships and expand sanctions to a target's environment.[204]

Coordination on the above efforts is already happening multilaterally, but its scope and scale should be significantly expanded. For example, a report on the implementation of Magnitsky sanctions examined the activities of the United States, Canada, the United Kingdom, and the European Union (EU), and found that only "11 percent of Magnitsky sanctions have been multilateralized by two or more jurisdictions."[205] It also found that civil society input into sanctions was uneven, with 34 percent of US-imposed sanctions informed by civil society, compared with only 13 percent of EU-imposed sanctions.[206] It further observed significant discrepancies in geographic regions targeted for sanctions, willingness of states to sanction targets in an allied country, as well as the kinds of human rights abuse and victims that are most likely to generate sanctions.[207] Countries also showed significant variation in strategies, with some focused more on sanctioning individuals, while others showed greater emphasis on sanctioning corporate entities.

This variation raises the need for a more systematic approach, built on greater intelligence and research capacities, as well as clearer standards and consistency of application. A democratic alliance could operate as a de facto global sanctions coordinating body. In addition, criteria for sanctions could be expanded. Already human rights abuse and corruption are considered justifiable grounds for sanctions—perhaps undermining democracy may be included as additional grounds in the future.

JUDICIAL ACCOUNTABILITY

In addition to heightened monitoring to increase backfire and implement sanctions, democracies can also establish formal investigatory capacities to build dossiers on perpetrators for referral to relevant judicial bodies. When regime perpetrators know that the cloak of anonymity will be lifted—that they will likely be named, personally sanctioned, and referred for criminal prosecution—it could have a deterrent effect.

While individual criminal responsibility for human rights violation is a relatively undeveloped area of international law, there are several potential mechanisms that can be used to bring officials committing human rights abuses to justice.[208]

First, the International Criminal Court was established in 1998 by treaty as a body to hold accountable those who commit the most serious international crimes: genocide, war crimes, crimes against humanity, and the crime of aggression.

Second, ad hoc international tribunals are also an option to hold accountable those who engage in violent repression. These can be created through the UN, as well as by separate international agreements. Most often, such tribunals have been established after the resolution of a political conflict and with the consent of the impacted government, although they could be created without such consent. Their creation, or the threat thereof, may deter abuses during the course of a conflict.

Finally, national courts have been used as a mechanism for bringing to justice those responsible for human rights violations, under the theory of universal jurisdiction. The legal basis is that prosecutors in individual nations may bring cases against those committing human rights violations overseas, in furtherance of universally accepted, fundamental human rights. Over the last two decades, the number of universal jurisdiction cases has risen around the world. According to Trial International, sixteen countries have ongoing prosecutions, including a landmark case on torture and war crimes committed in Syria by a Regional Court in Germany.[209] Lithuania and Poland recently initiated criminal cases regarding crimes, human rights violations, and a plane hijacking in Belarus.

If a mechanism can be established in a particular case, a further challenge is for democracies to ensure that those engaged in violent repression are taken into custody and brought to justice. Democracies would need to establish a systematic approach for doing so. Notably, this effort could also play into an escalatory framework as discussed later in this chapter—whereby at certain thresholds of repression, greater resources would be allocated to automatically triggered investigations.

LEVERAGING CAPACITY FOR DEMOCRATIC MILITARY PERSUASION

Currently the US Department of Defense and the ministries of defense of several European allies have a number of well-established and effective programs under the category sometimes known as security sector reform (SSR) or as defense institution building (DIB). These programs help develop functional capabilities of armed forces in countries that have already made a commitment to democracy, and are designed "to empower partner nation defense institutions to establish or re-orient their policies and structures to make their defense sector more transparent, accountable, effective, affordable and responsive to civilian control."[210]

In contrast, there currently is a lack of well-developed concepts and programs to bring the influence of the armed forces of the democracies to bear on countries that remain autocratic. While democratic militaries have many points of contact with those of autocratic countries—through exchange and educational programs, delegations, joint exercises, and international conferences—there is neither training at the service war colleges, nor guidance in the instructions of DOD or defense ministries of allied nations, for the military officers of democratic countries to use their personal interactions for building support for democratic transitions.

Yet there are many specific ways in which military officers from democracies can both set an example and engage the thinking of their counterparts in authoritarian regimes, so that these officers are open to and supportive of, even if not instigating, democratic reform within their countries. There are substantial institutional and individual benefits to military service under a democratic government instead of an authoritarian one. Understanding these benefits, as well as the often-unspoken sources of dissatisfaction of serving under authoritarian rule, can help democratic service members engage more effectively in advancing democratic attitudes in their personal and professional interactions with foreign counterparts.

Former Admiral Dennis Blair has advocated this approach, including that US military officers should have a democracy "elevator speech" ready, and emphasizes that both a speech's substance and tone (which should be culturally sensitive) are important.[211] Over time, such efforts can shift attitudes and possibly decision-making of an autocrat's security forces, especially during moments when an autocrat is challenged by a movement.

In addition, when authoritarians crack down on movements, military and defense officials in democratic governments should leverage their extensive points of formal and informal contact to influence the decisions of their security forces. Blair states that during times of crisis:

> *Personal contacts among military officials and officers in democratic countries and military leaders in the autocratic and transitional countries will be important. The officer or official in the democracy with the most knowledge, friendships, and influence within the country in transition may have to be called from another assignment to work on the transition.*[212]

With preparation, such efforts can become proactive, systematic, and more coordinated among democracies internationally, and potentially tip the balance at key moments for pro-democracy movements.

DISRUPTING MALIGN INFLUENCE OPERATIONS

Democracies should increase their efforts to inhibit major propagators of authoritarianism, such as the governments of the People's Republic of China (PRC) and Russia, by disrupting their foreign influence operations. A growing body of work identifies various ways that authoritarians exert influence in other countries' politics as well as proven strategies for preventing and countering this malign influence. Evidence points to three tools—or areas of support—available for limiting malign influence, or at least mitigating its impact.[213]

First, democracies can provide support to activists to uncover, understand, and raise public awareness about the strategies and tactics foreign authoritarians use in each country to prop up a regime and expand their own influence inside the country's borders, and the impact of these efforts on vulnerable democracies. There is an already expansive set of case studies and comparative examinations on this topic, but country-specific work is required to make sure strategies are targeted and effective.[214] Conducting and widely sharing this research is proven to raise awareness across target countries of PRC activities and can help catalyze action against foreign influence efforts. To maximize impact, research must be widely disseminated within the country in question both within and outside government. Sharing evidence-based research on authoritarian influence efforts in a country can help raise awareness and generate political will to enact policy reforms to curb such foreign interference.

A second form of support involves equipping local stakeholders with the tools and resources to expose foreign malign influence; hold complicit leaders accountable; as well as devise and advocate for locally appropriate policy solutions to bolster democratic resilience and counter authoritarian influence. This work includes supporting local advocacy campaigns largely centered on raising awareness about the impact of the corrosive elements of authoritarian influence. US-funded work with this goal has been effective. In Cambodia, for instance, grants supported two environmental activist organizations to produce investigative documentaries on the impact of PRC-backed infrastructure projects on the environment. In Peru, a US-funded advocacy campaign led by a local partner exposed the impact of projects funded and implemented by China National Petroleum Corporation (CNPC) on Peru's Amazonian Indians and other Indigenous peoples. This research sparked a public outcry that led the Chinese embassy to enter into dialogue with impacted groups.

Finally, democracies can provide support to catalyze dialogue between stakeholders and policymakers on viable solutions to mitigate malign influence, and then hold officials accountable for implementing them. In Nigeria, US-funded projects supported developing a guidebook that helps Nigerian media stakeholders identify and expose PRC's influence in Nigeria with an emphasis on sharp power tactics used to influence Nigeria's media landscape. These interventions center on equipping local advocacy organizations with resources to analyze forms of PRC or Russian government interference and evidence-based policy options, based on comparable contexts, for preventing and mitigating this outside influence.

Constraining Authoritarian Behavior: A Tiered Response to Repression

To further deter authoritarian repression, democracies should develop a tiered framework for imposing costs in response to escalating domestic (and at times international) repression of civil resistance movements.

Determining what actions to take, when, and at what level, depends significantly on context, but clear standards and decision-making processes can help foster coordination and rapid response.

We offer a preliminary framework on page 85, and below we address relevant questions on how such a framework could be further developed and operationalized.

To whom would the framework apply?

The framework is designed to respond to repression of civil resistance movements, but movements would need to meet certain criteria to qualify. Two minimal standards are that: a movement is committed to nonviolent means; and the movement's goals are consistent with democracy and internationally recognized human rights.[215]

At what thresholds would a response be triggered?

Preliminarily, we have identified three tiers of repression that could trigger escalating international responses (see table on the following page). However, even if consensus

is achieved among democracies about criteria for each tier, these criteria would be subject to ongoing interpretation and revision. One reason for this is that authoritarians innovate, particularly in their use of "smart repression" strategies, which are repressive tactics that are less visible or less attributable to the regime, and thus less likely to generate domestic or international outrage. A notable subset of "smart" strategies is also preemptive repression, which is repression that is specifically designed to prevent an enabling environment for movements and thus prevent them from forming, while simultaneously minimizing any potential backlash. Examples of smart and preemptive repression include the use of laws and surveillance technologies that enable regimes to more precisely target dissidents with threats and administrative repression, which are often not publicly visible. Opening sham investigations can also be a remarkably effective form of attacking individuals and civil society organizations, draining their resources, consuming their time, inducing self-censorship, and deterring other organizations from political engagement—without generating widespread backlash. When people publicly mobilize, digital surveillance can also allow regimes to avoid high visibility violent crackdowns, since protesters can be identified and then arrested one-by-one in low visibility night raids in the ensuing days. Regimes also seek to organize or agitate civilian supporters to engage in acts of violence against civil resisters, while the regime claims it is uninvolved.

The impacts of these forms of repression can be severe, but they are designed to avoid overt red lines that regimes fear will generate backfire. Therefore, a tiered framework for calibrating democratic responses to authoritarian repression should consider both the particular act of repression and its functional effects, and thresholds must be regularly evaluated, since authoritarians will seek gray areas that muddle discrete categories.

What action(s) might be taken?

Responses to repression should be proportional—with lower costs for shutting down a small section of the internet or jailing a single leader (although to some extent, this depends on who the leader is), and more robust consequences for a regime that authorizes lethal military force against nonviolent demonstrators (e.g., the Syrian government in 2011), or jailing and torture of hundreds of movement participants.

However, before actions are confirmed, movements should be consulted as well, since various interventions can have wide-ranging effects that affect not just a regime, but the population living under it. Democracies should listen and then act, seeking to be an extension of a movement's strategy and leverage, rather than a substitute for it.

In addition, strategic considerations must also be factored, based on what forms of action are deemed most likely to change the target's behavior. However, in some cases imposing a cost may be needed even if it is deemed unlikely to change the target's behavior in the short term, since actions also have a signaling function and create demonstration effects for other regimes. Threats must be credible to be believed, and this depends on the consistency with which consequences are applied.

Would democratic states agree to take action?

In addition to the above factors, democracies inevitably will weigh potential escalatory responses against their other national interests before decisions are made. In most cases, there will be trade-offs, and some policymakers may argue for the subordination of democracy, human rights, and countering authoritarianism to other national interests. Yet at times in the past, this trade-off has also significantly contributed to long-term threats, and damaged democratic credibility, which has weakened the overall position of democracies in the world. A reevaluation is due.

Framework for Tiered Response		
Repression Level	**Repression Characteristics (some or all listed characteristics may apply)**	**Potential Actions**
Level One	• Disruption of movement operations. • Jailing movement members.	• Warning of reevaluation of security cooperation, trade, and aid relationships. • Strong diplomatic statements, including threats of personal (i.e. Magnitsky) sanctions against regime officials.
Level Two	• Sustained disruption of movement operations. • Broader jailing of movement members. • Credible reports of torture to movement members in jails. • Deaths of several movement members.	• Revaluation of security cooperation and restrictions on technology exports. • Pressure on other regimes to withdraw support, and restrict security cooperation. • Economic sanctions on regime members and enablers. • Consideration of broader economic sanctions.
Level Three	• Widespread jailing of movement members. • Widespread killing of movement members.	• Broaden and deepen sanctions. • Secondary pressures against allies of the perpetrating regimes. • Removal from SWIFT network.* • Cyberattacks to disrupt regime coercive apparatus. • Derecognition. • Arrest and jail regime authorities.

*SWIFT STANDS FOR SOCIETY FOR WORLDWIDE INTERBANK FINANCIAL TELECOMMUNICATION.

LEVEL ONE: REGIME DISRUPTING MOVEMENT ORGANIZING, DETAINING SEVERAL MOVEMENT MEMBERS

Scenario: An authoritarian regime is limiting a movement's ability to organize, disrupting its financial and communications infrastructure, and jails several of a movement's members. The regime also deploys security forces to use less lethal forms of repression against public acts of civil resistance.

Potential response: A standard US and allied response at this level of repression would include reevaluating existing security cooperation, trade, and aid relationships. Personal (i.e., Magnitsky) sanctions could be threatened against regime officials and key enablers.

The authoritarian would be informed that international monitoring and investigatory capacities will now engage in heighted focus on the regime's activities.

Diplomacy would also be used. The United States and allies would publicly condemn the authoritarian's actions. If the regime uses smart repression tactics, they should be highlighted and their impacts on people's lives should be emphasized in order to maximize outrage. If the movement consents, democratic governments may also express their support for the movement's goals.

Democracies would also make clear what additional costs the regime and its backers would face should they escalate repression further, and reserve the right to escalate their response if recent regime actions do not desist or reverse.

LEVEL TWO: REGIME INTIMIDATING, PHYSICALLY HARMING, AND ACTIVELY DETAINING MOVEMENT MEMBERS

Scenario: An authoritarian regime is using more drastic repression techniques including intimidating and physically harming movement members. The government is jailing large numbers of movement participants and disrupting remaining members' ability to organize by cutting off internet or other communications channels. Torture is selectively used on jailed movements participants. As mobilization increases, several movement members die, although the regime claims that their killings were "justified" or denies a role in their death.

Potential response: Existing security cooperation to the authoritarian regime would be revoked. Technology exports would be restricted. Allies of the regime would also receive pressure to withdraw their support.

The authoritarian would be informed that international monitoring and investigatory capacities will now receive additional resources to focus on the regime's activities with the intent of building a case for potential criminal referrals. Specific perpetrators of abuse would be named.

Personal sanctions against regime elites and entities involved in repression would be leveled, as well as identified enablers, with consideration of stronger economic coercion to further squeeze the regime's finances.

The United States and allies would consider immediately removing the regime from the SWIFT network, while also considering possible impacts on the civilian population. Removal from SWIFT denies banks access to international markets, delaying or making it impossible for a government to receive payments for exports. This can stop inflow of profits from commodities or other exports, limiting a regime's cash reserves and the personal coffers of its leaders and enablers. With adequate planning and preparation, such removal would happen quickly as punishment for violent repression of democratic movements, rather than slowly ratcheting up and combining packages of sanctions, as has previously been the norm.

The United States and allies would also balance using economic coercion to punish or deter behavior with employing measures to incentivize and reward improvements in behavior. This can involve offering more favorable trade terms—like removing tariffs or barriers on goods—in exchange for agreement to enact democratic reforms. The conditions (if any) under which personal sanctions may be lifted should be communicated. Following sustained improvements, the United States and others could also consider bilateral trade agreements on a finite number of areas.

LEVEL THREE: WIDESPREAD DETENTION AND KILLINGS

Scenario: An authoritarian regime is actively suppressing a movement, widely detaining its members, with routine use of torture, and killing activists. Large-scale protests have been met with deadly force by regime military or police.

Potential response: This is the thorniest challenge and one the United States and allies have most often fallen short in effectively addressing. Absent viable options or clear benchmarks on what to do, the United States has repeatedly ratcheted up rhetoric and sanctions, but these have been unable to stop certain autocrats from committing sustained and widespread violence against their populations. In these instances—from the Lukashenko regime

Tunisian flags hang on a door during a protest against President Kais Saied's referendum on a new constitution, in Tunis, Tunisia, July 23, 2022. REUTERS/Zoubeir Souissi

seeking to crush its opposition, the Assad regime's atrocities against nonviolent demonstrators, the Iranian government's repeated repression of popular movements for rights and democracy, and the Myanmar military junta's killing of protesters—the standard set of economic and diplomatic tools have proven insufficient to change such state behavior.

Options that can escalate pressure further include imposing costs—including personalized sanctions, potentially broader forms of economic pressure, and heightened investigations into aiding and abetting repression—on a widening net of state allies and nonstate enablers of the authoritarian regime in question.

Official derecognition of the abusive regime in some cases could also be an option.[216] In such a case, it is deemed that the autocrat has abdicated the responsibility of sovereignty by vastly violating the population's human rights, and the population has made it clear through their mobilization that they are exercising self-determination to seek different leadership for their country.[217] The impact of derecognition is strengthened when multiple states derecognize the abusive regime and simultaneously recognize a credible alternative leadership, which

may be in exile. If so, the nation's embassies and funds held abroad would be made available to the alternative leadership, and resources would be directed to them to increase their capacity for planning a political transition. The derecognized autocrat would also no longer have sovereign immunity, and could face potential arrest for their criminal behavior.

Democracies may also consider using cyber tools, applying general principles to determine their use. First and foremost, democracies should consult with movements on what they think would be helpful—we should listen and seek to do no harm. Second, cyber tools might be employed to disrupt infrastructure and other sectors and not destroy them, so as not to constitute an act of war. Finally, democracies would use cyber tactics to reduce or remove resources regimes rely on for repression. Specific options include using cyberattacks—i.e., denial of service attacks—to disrupt regime access to financial accounts; disable or disrupt military planning or weapons systems; and deter further escalation in repression. Using cyber tactics in this fashion provides deniability to help avoid escalation while possibly mitigating regime repression and thereby aiding movements.

Pillar III: Policy Recommendations

Recommendation #7: Establish a new entity of leading democracies.

- **Democratic governments should establish a new coordinating entity for advancing democracy.** A new coordinating mechanism, established through the G7 or a new coalition of democracies, could spearhead a campaign to empower democratic movements around the world. This should include moral, legal, and financial assistance to people who are on the ground working to advance democracy and under the threat of retribution by authoritarian regimes or their local proxies. The new entity would also act as an active repository of research and analysis to identify targets for sanctions, and to harmonize their implementation.

Recommendation #8: Establish a mechanism to hold accountable regime officials involved in the suppression of democracy.

- Democratic governments should **establish an internal mechanism to investigate and document unlawful or illegitimate actions taken by officials in authoritarian regimes that violently repress civil resistance movements.** Such a mechanism can be housed within the justice ministries or investigative bureaus of these governments.

- Democracies should **join together within a multilateral framework to hold accountable such officials.**

Recommendation #9: Assign defense agencies to take a more active role in democracy support.

- Democratic governments should **assign their respective departments or ministries of defense with taking a more active role in democracy support.** Defense officials and military officers from democracies should seek to influence their counterparts in autocratic countries to support democratic change and strengthening in their own countries. When authoritarians crack down on movements, military and defense officials in democratic governments should redouble such efforts.

Recommendation #10: Develop a systematic framework with escalating responses to deter violent repression.

- **The United States should establish a government-wide working group to develop a tiered framework of escalating responses to violent repression.** The United States should work with leading democracies to build a framework for collective action centered around enforcement of this tiered approach.

- **Other leading democracies should establish a similar mechanism**, and ensure that these efforts are coordinated.

Recommendation #11: Scale up funding to counter foreign malign influence.

- **The United States should scale up funding dedicated to countering foreign malign influence in third countries**. Funding should center on increasing the resilience of governments and civil society against attempts by authoritarian governments such as the PRC and the Russian government—the two most powerful actors opposed to democracy worldwide—to erode democracy and coopt elites.

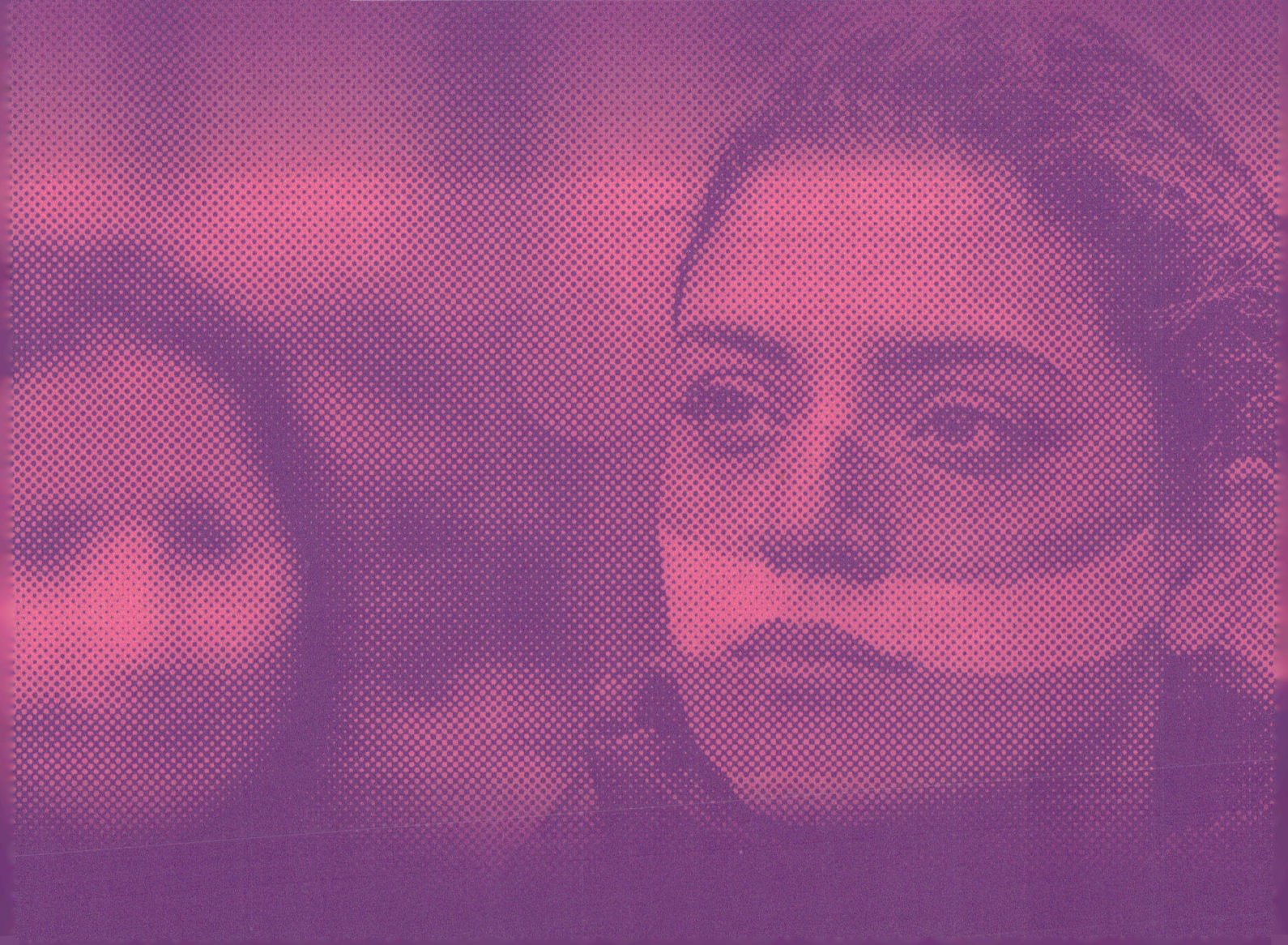

6. Addressing Questions About Implementation

When lives hang in the balance, any model of external assistance for democracy and human rights must be subject to scrutiny. This section identifies questions and potential concerns about international support for movements, and establishing a right to assistance. These include:

1. Is support for civil resistance synonymous with supporting regime change?

2. Can external support undermine civil resistance movements?

3. What if external support to a movement contributes to societal instability?

4. How should support for civil resistance be balanced with other national interests in foreign policy?

5. How would a right to assistance be established? Would the norm be formally invoked?

6. What if authoritarians try to weaponize a right to assistance against democracies?

Much of the substance of responding to these concerns is included in this playbook already, but here we conclude by addressing these concerns directly.

1. IS SUPPORT FOR CIVIL RESISTANCE SYNONYMOUS WITH SUPPORTING REGIME CHANGE?[218]

Supporting civil resistance movements seeking democracy and human rights is a policy of human rights and democracy support, not a policy of externally driven regime change. This is so for three reasons:

- Movement participants are exercising their human rights through nonviolent mobilization.

- The movements in question have goals consistent with international human rights.

- Participants in these movements have a right to request and receive assistance.

Unsurprisingly, for nearly two decades, authoritarians have characterized these movements as "color revolutions," a pejorative term that seeks to cast them as foreign-sponsored, regime-change efforts. This framing is deliberately designed to shift conversation away from human rights and the fact that civil resistance movements are indigenously driven by the energy, grievances, and aspirations of populations living under oppressive rule. The authoritarian frame of "color revolutions" is self-serving, and must be soundly rejected by democracies.

In civil resistance movements, decisions about what objectives to pursue and what actions to take are made by participants on the ground, rather than foreign supporters. These movements cannot be commanded and controlled from the outside. Furthermore, such movements have a wide range of possible goals (many are reformist or rights-based in nature) and do not exclusively seek political transitions.

That said, some movements seek democratic transitions, and it is their right to do so. Often these movements start by trying to achieve reformist goals, but when their efforts are met by an autocrat's brutality, corruption, and incompetence, they start to seek a change of government altogether. In such circumstances, the choice is made by the movement itself, not a foreign actor. The choice is also shaped by the actions of an autocrat—reforms and compromises may have preserved the autocrat's rule, but obstinacy and abuse instead led to a transformation of popular demands.

2. CAN EXTERNAL SUPPORT UNDERMINE CIVIL RESISTANCE MOVEMENTS?[219]

It can be challenging for well-intentioned external actors to discern what exact support to provide to a movement, as well as where, when, how, and to which particular groups to provide it. Movements are generally less structured than traditional nongovernmental organizations, may have unclear lines of leadership and accountability, and depend on popular voluntary mobilization in order to succeed. There is always a possibility that external support could damage a movement, for example by reducing its legitimacy, increasing the risk of repression, or causing internal divisions among groups within it. For precisely this reason, in chapter 3 we emphasize that external actors need to develop a movement mindset to navigate local contexts.

Although there is no single or simple formula for effective support, principles of external support discussed in this playbook can ameliorate concerns about contamination, as discussed below.

Listen to the Needs of Mobilized Communities

External actors should begin by seeking to understand the context in which they may become involved. Because civil resistance is a bottom-up phenomenon, external actors must make efforts to identify and listen to multiple and diverse grassroots groups. Any assistance should be tailored to expressed needs from people on the ground, rather than imposed.

If movement participants feel the risk of support from an external government is too high, they may not request any support. In other cases they may request indirect forms of assistance, such as support for research or generalized efforts to share information in a particular language in a particular region of the world. Other options include requesting specific support through nonstate actors, such as international nongovernmental organizations (advocacy or philanthropy), diaspora populations, or local CSOs. On the other hand, some movements may also request visible and direct action by democracies on a particular issue.

Notably, some of the most impactful forms of movement support are often low key and minimally interventionist, such as information sharing, and so a policy of movement support may not require large-scale public efforts in order to be effective in some circumstances.

Support Local Ownership and Empowerment

Local actors lead nonviolent movements. They have the deepest knowledge of their situation, bear the most risk, and have the most invested in the outcome. Therefore, external support should be an extension of local efforts, rather than a substitute for them. External actors need to be flexible and possibly give up a certain amount of control, allowing on-the-ground partners and recipients to use external support in the ways that they feel are most needed.

Avoid Advocating for a Particular Course of Action

Outsiders can share case studies, research findings, and planning tools and engage in Socratic dialogue with activists about prioritizing various tactics. However, because outsiders lack sufficient local knowledge, they should not advocate for particular courses of action. A single exception to this is that external actors should feel comfortable advising against the use of violence. Violence is empirically proven to be counterproductive, and the benefits of nonviolent tactics are well-established by a growing body of practice and research.

Coordinate Support with Other External Actors

Integrating efforts with other external actors is often necessary to maximize impact. There are many different forms of support that can be provided, a variety of providers and recipients of such support, and numerous other considerations such as timing and the local context. Movements have diverse needs and different external actors may be best suited to support a movement's changing needs over time.

Do No Harm, through Action or Inaction

In consultation with trusted local groups, external actors should consider the risks of harm due to both action *and* inaction. In some cases, where external actors are getting mixed signals from the grassroots or insufficient input, it might be wise to abstain from assertive action and instead gather more information (for example about the degree to which certain external assistance may impact other local actors) or wait for the situation to ripen.

In other cases, if multiple trusted groups are actively waging civil resistance and ask for support, external actors should consider responding favorably, even if the request is unexpected or on short notice. Local actors can determine what level of risk they are willing to tolerate, and sometimes failure by external actors to respond assertively to their requests can result in harm.

3. WHAT IF EXTERNAL SUPPORT CONTRIBUTES TO SOCIETAL INSTABILITY?[220]

Concerns may be raised that support for civil resistance can increase societal instability, and therefore the risk of civil war. For example, two countries—Syria and Yemen—experienced nonviolent movements in 2011 and subsequently succumbed to violent conflict. In Syria, the nonviolent opposition was overcome by a violent flank that rapidly developed into an insurgency; in Yemen, civil resis-

Teachers, health workers, retirees and public employees protest against the government of Venezuela's President Nicolas Maduro, in Maracay, Venezuela August 23, 2022. The banner reads "The fight (continues)." REUTERS/Gaby Oraa

tance led to an environment where opposition groups began to press their claims with violence. These cases point to a disturbing fact: for all the promise that civil resistance can lead to democratic transitions, there is a subset of cases that highlights a major risk.

The research bears this out. Scholars Chenoweth and Stephan find that within ten years after a national civil resistance campaign (either successful or failed) there is a 28 percent chance of civil war onset. In contrast, within ten years after a violent campaign (either successful or failed) there is a 42 percent chance of civil war onset.[221] While the probability of civil war after a violent campaign is significantly higher, the 28 percent probability after a nonviolent campaign calls for further attention.

However, external actors *do not control the timing of civil resistance movements*. These movements emerge from a population's deep-seated resentment against the repression, misrule, lack of accountability, incompetence, corruption, and inequality that characterize authoritarian rule. When populations find authoritarian rule intolerable and start to rise up and resist (this is more a question of *when*,

not *if*), they face a pivotal choice of how they will resist: through violent or nonviolent tactics.

In light of this, external support should seek to incentivize and support nonviolent strategies and tactics, which keep the conflict trajectory as close as possible to having a democratic outcome, and as far as possible from resulting in civil war. In this way, effective forms of external support can mitigate the risk of violent conflict. As policy experts Stephan, Sadaf Lakhani, and Nadia Naviwala write:

> *Because outside actors probably will not be able to prevent people from engaging in protest or other direct action, particularly if they are suffering acute grievances, to minimize risk of violent instability they could invest in helping civil societies develop the capacity to organize nonviolently and maintain nonviolent discipline.*[222]

Thus, risk of instability that devolves into civil war is inherent in the authoritarian model of governance. What seems to be relative "peace" at the surface of nondemocratic regimes obscures the suppression of pent up demand for change, which eventually gets triggered. The question then is how incentivizing civil resistance might compare with alternative options. Inaction by external actors may seem to have the lowest risk at any given point in time, but lack of support for civil resistance may result in heightened volatility in the future. Without the benefit of public educational efforts and capacity-building support, people may think violence is the only realistic option available to them, and a nascent nonviolent campaign may transition to violent insurgency.

4. HOW SHOULD SUPPORT FOR CIVIL RESISTANCE BE BALANCED WITH OTHER NATIONAL INTERESTS IN FOREIGN POLICY?

These is no single answer to this question—context matters enormously. However, a burden of proof does not rest only with those who seek to elevate democracy and human rights in foreign policy decision-making.

Research on the relationship between civil resistance and democratic development consistently shows that civil resistance movements are one of the primary factors in driving democratic gains and ending authoritarian rule. Democracies should not delude themselves about these facts, or the trade-offs they make when they prioritize other interests in their bilateral relations with autocratic regimes.

Lastly, support for civil resistance can also help extricate democracies from such binary foreign policy choices. For example, trade relations and security cooperation do not necessarily preclude offering impactful support to civil society, directly or indirectly.

5. HOW WOULD A RIGHT TO ASSISTANCE BE ESTABLISHED? WOULD THE NORM BE FORMALLY INVOKED?

International law derives from both treaties and customs. This playbook lays out a rationale for the R2A norm based on treaty law. In a more democratic world, this norm could be argued and put up for a vote in the United Nations, but this is politically impossible amid the current autocratic wave.

However, the norm can still be further advanced through practice. The kinds of movement-support activities outlined in this playbook are justified by the norm. Simultaneously engaging in those activities further strengthens the norm.

Next steps in establishing a right to assistance would entail democracies coming together to discuss its bases, fostering shared commitment to minimal standards that

they expect all governments to meet regarding the rights of their populations to receive assistance, and then acting accordingly. Because the activities to support the norm are generally not highly interventionist, formal invocation of the norm would not be needed in most cases. In addition, the establishment of the norm may not require a formal declaration regarding particular countries. Rather, establishment may happen as democracies consistently set the precedent, in word and deed, that certain lines matter for them.

Over time, sustained democratic practice and coordination on this norm may also lead to the creation of more formal oversight and invocation bodies.

6. WHAT IF AUTHORITARIANS TRY TO WEAPONIZE A RIGHT TO ASSISTANCE AGAINST DEMOCRACIES?

As authoritarians seek to close off their societies to democratic influence, they simultaneously exploit democratic openness to further their foreign agendas. They have done this throughout the entire seventeen-year autocratic wave, and we expect that they will continue to try to do so, regardless of whether democracies assert a right to assistance or not.

The right to assistance can level the playing field. Democracies already allow a great deal of foreign influence within our borders. Therefore, when democracies speak to other countries about allowing their populations to receive support, the values and actions of democracies are already aligned.

However, we recognize that authoritarians would still try to cite a right to assistance as a pretext to promote destabilization of states. We think the norm still significantly favors democracies, for several reasons.

First, two criteria for supporting movements under the right to assistance are that a movement is committed to nonviolent means and that the movement's goals are consistent with democracy and internationally recognized human rights. Those criteria could be expanded and refined in the future.

We further offered guidance on how to determine if a movement is nonviolent for the purposes of the norm:

By relying on indicators such as a movement's core principles, statements from movement leaders, the content of movement trainings, and the practices of the vast majority of movement participants, a movement's nonviolent character can be discerned.

Women, with their faces painted in the colors of Iran's flag, take part in a protest by Iranian community members to show solidarity with Iranian people, in Brussels, Belgium, February 20, 2023. REUTERS/Johanna Geron

These parameters ensure that movements eligible for support are those that are committed to nonviolent means as a method of making change—and that demonstrate that commitment in multiple ways. This distinguishes them from movements that are more characteristically authoritarian—which may opportunistically use nonviolent tactics, but also tend to threaten violence if they do not get their way.

A second factor in the norm that favors democracies is that, as discussed in chapter 4, international human rights law also allows certain limits on a right to assistance, and these limits would mitigate against authoritarian influence.

Third, as discussed in chapter 2, research on diffusion of civil resistance movements finds that authoritarian governments are much more vulnerable to the spread of civil resistance than democracies. Thus, authoritarians have more to be concerned about when it comes to allowing the free flow of information and resources to their civil societies than democracies do. This also validates the view that domestic populations must be sufficiently aggrieved and motivated to wage civil resistance against a government: authoritarians know this, and fear it.

Lastly, civil resistance movements are composed of thousands or millions of people who make the personal decision to take action and mobilize (sometimes with significant sacrifice of their time, energy, material resources, and personal safety). Popular legitimacy of goals, actions, and communications is critical for this to happen—a movement has to represent people's grievances and aspirations or else people stop supporting it. If at the behest of an autocrat, a movement adopts an agenda that does not resonate domestically, public participation will rapidly decline. When a movement starts to follow a foreign agenda, its popular legitimacy—and thus its popular participation—is likely to decrease. Therefore, civil resistance movements can wither if they succumb to foreign control, and this may limit some foreign efforts to "weaponize" them. Indeed, foreign support that attempts to manipulate a movement may be more likely to cause the movement to fail altogether, rather than achieve a foreigner's aims (unless those aims are, in fact, to produce failure).

About the Authors

Hardy Merriman is President of the International Center on Nonviolent Conflict (ICNC), a Nonresident Senior Fellow in the Atlantic Council's Scowcroft Center for Strategy and Security, and was a Principal Investigator (PI) on the Fostering a Fourth Democratic Wave Project.

He has worked in the field of civil resistance for over two decades, presenting at workshops for activists and organizers from around the world; developing programs and grantmaking for practitioners and scholars; publishing commentary; and speaking widely about civil resistance movements with academics, journalists, and members of international organizations.

In addition to his leadership of the International Center on Nonviolent Conflict, he also taught as an adjunct lecturer at the Fletcher School of Law and Diplomacy at Tufts University from 2016-8.

His writings have been translated into numerous languages. Recent publications include coauthoring the book *Glossary of Civil Resistance: A Resource for Study and Translation of Key Terms* (2021), and the report "Preventing Mass Atrocities: From a Responsibility to Protect (RtoP) to a Right to Assist (RtoA) Campaigns of Civil Resistance" (2019).

Patrick Quirk, Ph.D. is Vice President for Strategy, Innovation, and Impact at the International Republican Institute (IRI), a non-partisan organization dedicated to supporting democracy worldwide. In this role, Dr. Quirk provides the leadership, management, and vision to ensure that IRI is addressing global challenges to democracy by developing innovative and evidence-based programs, tools, and resources. Concurrent to serving at IRI, Dr. Quirk is a Nonresident Senior Fellow in the Atlantic Council's Scowcroft Center for Strategy and Security and an Adjunct Professor at Georgetown University. From 2019-2021, he was a Nonresident Fellow in the Foreign Policy Program of the Brookings Institution.

Before joining IRI, Dr. Quirk served on the U.S. Secretary of State's Policy Planning staff in the Department of State as the lead advisor for fragile states, conflict and stabilization, and foreign assistance. Prior to Policy Planning, he served in State's Bureau of Conflict and Stabilization Operations (CSO) as Senior Advisor for Policy and Strategy. During his government service, Dr. Quirk received several Superior and Meritorious Honor Awards.

Prior to joining the Department of State, he was a Research Fellow at the German Marshall Fund as well as designed and implemented conflict prevention and democracy strengthening foreign assistance interventions overseas. His analysis has appeared in Foreign Policy, the Financial Times, The National Interest, NPR, and Real Clear Defense, among other outlets. Dr. Quirk earned a B.A. in History from Bates College and a Ph.D. in Political Science from Johns Hopkins University.

Ash Jain is director for democratic order with the Scowcroft Center for Strategy and Security, where he oversees the Atlantic Council's Democratic Order Initiative and D-10 Strategy Forum. His work focuses on strengthening cooperation among democracies and advancing a rules-based, democratic order. He previously served as a member of the secretary of state's policy planning staff, focusing on US alliances and partnerships, international norms, and challenges to the democratic order — including those posed by Russia, China, Iran, and North Korea. Mr. Jain was a Bosch public policy fellow with the German Marshall Fund Transatlantic Academy and executive director for the Project for a United and Strong America, where he coordinated a bipartisan foreign policy task force to produce a blueprint for a values-based national security strategy. He also served as an adviser for the White House Office of Global Communications and with the Senate Committee on Homeland Security and Governmental Affairs. Mr. Jain has also taught as an adjunct professor at Georgetown University's School of Foreign Service. He earned a JD/MS in foreign service from Georgetown University and a BA in political science from the University of Michigan.

Acknowledgments

The authors would like to dedicate this publication to the late Dr. Peter Ackerman, former Founding Chair of the International Center on Nonviolent Conflict (ICNC). A long-time scholar and supporter of the field of civil resistance, this playbook builds on work that he produced and enabled. Peter championed civil resistance movements for decades and was a strong proponent of this project in particular.

The authors are deeply grateful to Damon Wilson who also inspired this project and helped facilitate its launch while executive vice president of the Atlantic Council.

The authors further express their gratitude to other colleagues at the Atlantic Council and the International Center on Nonviolent Conflict for their support. Matthew Kroenig, senior director of the Scowcroft Center for Strategy and Security has provided invaluable guidance throughout this process. Ivan Marovic, executive director of ICNC, has been a steadfast thought partner. Special thanks go to Danielle Miller, assistant director of the Scowcroft Center for Strategy and Security, for her ongoing programmatic support since the project's inception.

Lastly, the authors are grateful for the many people who contributed input and feedback to the project, including the co-chairs of the task force established to guide this effort—Derek Mitchell, Lisbeth Pilegaard, and Daniel Twining—as well as other members of the task force, who graciously gave their time to participate in meetings, review drafts of the playbook, and provide their expert perspectives.

ENDNOTES

1   Two key studies include Erica Chenoweth and Maria J. Stephan, *Why Civil Resistance Works: The Strategic Logic of Nonviolent Conflict* (New York: Columbia University Press, 2011); and Jonathan Pinckney, *From Dissent to Democracy: The Promise and Perils of Civil Resistance Transitions* (New York: Oxford University Press, 2020).

2   Scholars Luca Tomini, Suzan Gibril & Venelin Bochev define autocratization as "an 'umbrella concept' encompassing several phenomena of change such as democratic regression/backsliding (when the core features of liberal democracy are eroded but no transition to autocratic regime occurs), democratic breakdown (where democracy collapses), or authoritarian deepening (when we observe the deepening of authoritarian characteristics in already autocratic regimes)." See Luca Tomini, Suzan Gibril & Venelin Bochev (2023) "Standing up against autocratization across political regimes: a comparative analysis of resistance actors and strategies," *Democratization*, 30:1, 119-138, DOI: 10.1080/13510347.2022.2115480.

3   Erica Chenoweth and Maria J. Stephan, "Drop Your Weapons: When and Why Civil Resistance Works," *Foreign Affairs* (2014).

4   Erica Chenoweth and Maria J. Stephan, *The Role of External Support in Nonviolent Campaigns: Poisoned Chalice or Holy Grail?*, (Washington, DC: ICNC Press), 2.

5   Civil resistance can also be referred to as "nonviolent action," "people power," "political defiance," and "civic mobilization."

6   Steven Levitsky and Daniel Ziblatt, *How Democracies Die* (New York: Broadway Books, 2018), 217; and Stephen Haggard and Robert R. Kaufman, *Dictators and Democrats: Masses, Elites, and Regime Change* (Princeton, New Jersey: Princeton University Press, 2016), 337.

7   Timur Kuran, "Sparks and Prairie Fires: A Theory of Unanticipated Political Revolution," *Public Choice* (1989), 41-74; and Timur Kuran, "Now Out of Never: The Element of Surprise in the East European Revolution of 1989," *World Politics* (1991), 7-48.

8   Haggard and Kaufman, *Dictators and Democrats*, 19; and Jonathan Pinckney, *How to Win Well: Civil Resistance Breakthroughs and the Path to Democracy,* Special Report, International Center on Nonviolent Conflict (ICNC), April 2021, https://www.nonviolent-conflict.org/resource/how-to-win-well/.

9   Jonathan Pinckney, *When Civil Resistance Succeeds: Building Democracy After Popular Nonviolent Uprisings*, Monograph series (Washington, DC: ICNC Press, 2018).

10   Erica Chenoweth, "The Future of Nonviolent Resistance," *Journal of Democracy* 31, no. 3 (2020), 69-84.

11   Chenoweth, and Stephan, *Why Civil Resistance Works*, 213-15.

12   Chenoweth, and Stephan, *Why Civil Resistance Works*, 216.

13   Adrian Karatnycky and Peter Ackerman, *How Freedom Is Won: From Civic Resistance to Durable Democracy* (Washington, DC: Freedom House, 2005).

14   The noncivil resistance transitions examined in this study include top-down transitions but also transitions driven by violence and other means. See Pinckney, *When Civil Resistance Succeeds.*

15   Petter G. Johnstad, "Nonviolent Democratization: A Sensitivity Analysis of How Transition Mode and Violence Impact the Durability of Democracy," *Peace & Change* (2010), 464-482.

16   Markus Bayer, Felix S. Bethke, and Daniel Lambach, "The Democratic Dividend of Nonviolent Resistance," *Journal of Peace Research* (2016), 758-771.

17   Daniel Lambach et al., *Nonviolent Resistance and Democratic Consolidation* (Cham, Switzerland: Palgrave Macmillan, 2020), 50-53.

18   Felix S. Bethke and Jonathan Pinckney, "Non-violent Resistance and the Quality of Democracy," *Conflict Management and Peace Science* (2021), 503-523.

19   Judith Stoddard "How Do Major, Violent and Nonviolent Opposition Campaigns Impact Predicted Life Expectancy at Birth?," *Stability: International Journal of Security and Development* (2013).

20   Chenoweth and Stephan, *Why Civil Resistance Works*, 66.

21   See, for example, Eleanor Marchant, "Enabling Environments for Civic Movements and the Dynamics of Democratic Transition," Freedom House, July 2008, https://freedomhouse.org/sites/default/files/2022-02/Special_Report_Enabling_Environments_for_Civic_Movements_2008.pdf; Chenoweth and Stephan, *Why Civil Resistance Works*, 62-82; and Erica Chenoweth and Jay Ulfelder, "Can Structural Conditions Explain the Onset of Nonviolent Uprisings?," *Journal of Conflict Resolution* (2017), 298-324.

22   Chenoweth and Stephan, "Drop Your Weapons."

23   Political parties can also be considered part of civil society, but in this study they are examined as distinct from other civil society organizations.

24   Melis G. Laebens and Anna Lührmann, "What Halts Democratic Erosion? The Changing Role of Accountability," *Democratization* 28, no. 5 (2021), 908-928, DOI: 10.1080/13510347.2021.1897109.

25   Miguel Angel Lara Otaola, "Worried About the State of Democracy? Here Are Some Reasons to Be Optimistic Instead," Analysis, *Washington Post*, March 2, 2022, https://www.washingtonpost.com/politics/2022/03/02/democracy-backsliding-authoritarianism-index/.

26   Haggard and Kaufman, *Dictators and Democrats*, 357-358.

27   Laebens and Lührmann, "What Halts Democratic Erosion?," 26.

28   Samuel P. Huntington, "Democracy's Third Wave," *Journal of Democracy* (1991), 12-34.

29   George Papuashvili, "Post-World War I Comparative Constitutional Developments in Central and Eastern Europe," *International Journal of Constitutional Law* (2017), 137-172.

30   Samuel P. Huntington, *The Third Wave: Democratization in the Late Twentieth Century* (Norman, Oklahoma: University of Oklahoma Press, 1991), 17.

31   Huntington, *The Third Wave*, 18.

32   Anna Lührmann, "Disrupting the Autocratization Sequence: Towards Democratic Resilience," *Democratization* (2021): 1027.

33   Huntington, *The Third Wave*, 12.

34   David Strang, "Global Patterns of Decolonization, 1500-1987," *International Studies Quarterly* (1991): 429-454.

35   Huntington, *The Third Wave*, 13-31.

36   Huntington, *The Third Wave*, 13-31.

37   Larry Diamond, "Is the Third Wave of Democratization Over?: The Imperative of Consolidation," Kellogg Institute, Working Paper #237, 1997.

38   Larry Diamond, *Ill Winds: Saving Democracy from Russian Rage, Chinese Ambition, and American Complacency* (New York: Penguin Press, 2019), 54.

39   Evie Papada and Staffan I. Lindberg (eds.), *Democracy Report 2023: Defiance in the Face of Autocratization*, V-Dem Institute, University of Gothenburg, 2023, 6, 11. The use of the word "approximately" in this paragraph acknowledges that democracy classifications are not exact, and that different definitions and methodologies will reach different conclusions about the exact numbers of governments that fit into these respective categories. In particular, determining the point at which an "electoral democracy" shifts downward to the category of "electoral autocracy" is sensitive to various measures and interpretations. By referencing data on democracy and authoritarianism found in various reports, we are using the data as approximate benchmarks and to examine trends, but are not endorsing any particular classification of a country's government found in such reports.

40   Huntington, *The Third Wave*, 45-46.

41   Larry Diamond, *The Spirit of Democracy: The Struggle to Build Free Societies throughout the World* (New York: Times Books, 2008), 52-53.

42   Karatnycky and Ackerman, *How Freedom Is Won*.

43   Diamond, *The Spirit of Democracy*, 6.

44   Diamond, *The Spirit of Democracy*, 9.

45   Huntington, *The Third Wave*, 21.

46   Kuran, "Now Out of Never," 7.

47   Kuran, "Now Out of Never," 7-8.

48   Christian Caryl, "Who Brought Down the Berlin Wall?," *Foreign Policy*, November 5, 2009.

49   Michael McFaul, "Transitions from Postcommunism," *Journal of Democracy* 16, no. 3 (2005), 6.

50   McFaul, "Transitions from Postcommunism," 6.

51   Diamond, *Ill Winds*, 46.

52   For example, in 1984, Samuel Huntington wrote: "The substantial power of anti-democratic governments (particularly the Soviet Union), the unreceptivity to democracy of several major cultural traditions, the difficulties of eliminating poverty in large parts of the world, and the prevalence of high levels of polarization and violence in many societies all suggest that, with a few exceptions, the limits of democratic development in the world may well have been reached." Samuel P. Huntington, "Will More Countries Become Democratic?," *Political Science Quarterly*, 193-218, as cited in Diamond, *The Spirit of Democracy*, 10.

53   Larry Diamond, "Democracy's Arc: From Resurgent to Imperiled," Expanded Edition, *Journal of Democracy* (2022).

54   Anna Lührmann and Staffan I. Lindberg, "A Third Wave of Autocratization Is Here: What Is New About It?," *Democratization* (2019): 1097-1103.

55   Arch Puddington and Tyler Roylance, *Freedom in the World 2017: Populists and Autocrats: The Dual Threat to Global Democracy*, Freedom House, 2017, 4; and Yana Gorokhovskaia, Adrian Shahbaz and Amy Slipowitz, *Freedom in the World 2023: Marking 50 Years in the Struggle for Democracy*, Freedom House, 2023, 30.

56   Lührmann and Lindberg, "A Third Wave of Autocratization Is Here," 1102; and Larry Diamond, "Is the Third Wave Over?," *Journal of Democracy* (1996).

57   Vanessa A. Boese et al., "How Democracies Prevail: Democratic Resilience as a Two-stage Process," *Democratization* (2021): 885-907.

58   Philippe C. Schmitter and Terry Lynn Karl, "What Democracy Is...and Is Not," *Journal of Democracy* (1991): 78.

59   Francis Fukuyama, "Why Is Democracy Performing So Poorly?," *Journal of Democracy* (2015): 11-20.

60   Diamond, "Democracy's Arc," 17.

61   Kristian Skrede Gleditsch and Michael D. Ward, "Diffusion and the International Context of Democratization," *International Organization* (2006): 916.

62   Daniel Brinks and Michael Coppedge, "Diffusion Is No Illusion: Neighbor Emulation in the Third Wave of Democracy," *Comparative Political Studies* (2006): 463-489.

63   Boese et al., "How Democracies Prevail," 885-907.

64 Gleditsch and Ward, "Diffusion and the International Context of Democratization," 929.

65 Kristian S. Gleditsch and Mauricio Rivera, "The Diffusion of Nonviolent Campaigns," *Journal of Conflict Resolution* (2017): 1120-1145.

66 Gleditsch and Rivera, "The Diffusion of Nonviolent Campaigns," 1120-1145.

67 Kurt Weyland, "The Diffusion of Revolution: '1848' in Europe and Latin America," *International Organization* (2009): 391-423; and Kurt Weyland, "The Arab Spring: Why the Surprising Similarities with the Revolutionary Wave of 1848?" *Perspectives on Politics* (2012): 917-934.

68 Alex Braithwaite, Jessica Maves Braithwaite, and Jeffrey Kucik, "The Conditioning Effect of Protest History on the Emulation of Nonviolent Conflict," *Journal of Peace Research* (2015), 697-711.

69 For example, between 2004 and 2010, the International Center for Not-for-Profit Law (ICNL) found that "more than fifty countries considered or enacted measures restricting civil society." Moreover, between 2012 and 2015, "more than 120 laws constraining the freedoms of association and assembly...[were] proposed or enacted in 160 countries." See Douglas Rutzen, "Civil Society Under Assault," *Journal of Democracy* (2015): 30.

70 ICNL, *Defending the Right to Protest* (2022), https://www.icnl.org/post/analysis/defending-the-right-to-protest.

71 Douglas Rutzen, "Aid Barriers and the Rise of Philanthropic Protectionism," *International Journal of Not-for-Profit Law* (2015), https://www.icnl.org/resources/research/ijnl/aid-barriers-and-the-rise-of-philanthropic-protectionism.

72 Clement Voule, "UN Special Rapporteur Report on Assembly and Association Rights in the Digital Era, A/HRC/41/41," ICNL, https://www.icnl.org/post/report/un-special-rapporteurs-report-on-assembly-and-association-rights-in-the-digital-era. We appreciate the International Center for Not-for-Profit Law for contributing to this paragraph.

73 *Hearings on US Assistance to Promote Freedom and Democracy in Countries with Repressive Environments Before the House Appropriations Comm. State, Foreign Operations, and Relations Programs Subcomm.*, 113th Cong., Second Session (2014) (statement of Dr. Sarah E. Mendelson, deputy assistant administrator for democracy, conflict, and humanitarian assistance, US Agency for International Development), https://docs.house.gov/meetings/AP/AP04/20140226/101772/HHRG-113-AP04-Wstate-MendelsonS-20140226.pdf.

74 "Joint Statement of the Russian Federation and the People's Republic of China on the International Relations Entering a New Era and the Global Sustainable Development," February 5, 2022.

75 We appreciate the International Center for Not-for-Profit Law for contributing to this paragraph.

76 Lührmann and Lindberg, "A Third Wave of Autocratization Is Here," 1103.

77 Boese et al., "How Democracies Prevail," 885-907.

78 Boese et al., "How Democracies Prevail," 891-92.

79 Erica Chenoweth, "The Future of Nonviolent Resistance," 71.

80 Chenoweth, "The Future of Nonviolent Resistance," 75.

81 Chenoweth, "The Future of Nonviolent Resistance," 76-79.

82 Chenoweth, "The Future of Nonviolent Resistance," 78.

83 Isabel Ortiz et al., *World Protests: A Study of Key Protest Issues in the 21st Century* (Cham, Switzerland: Palgrave Macmillan, 2022).

84 Ortiz et al., *World Protests*, 3, 20, 27, 36, 44. Note that mobilizations with multiple grievances and demands are counted toward multiple categories above.

85 Ortiz et al., *World Protests*, 115.

86 Ortiz et al., *World Protests*, 68-69.

87 For example, the Task Force on US Strategy to Support Democracy and Counter Authoritarianism calls for democracy to become a "central tenet of domestic and foreign policy," requiring a "reordering of priorities, plans, and budgets," encompassing the country's "economic, social, technological, diplomatic, development, military, intelligence, and law enforcement" powers. See Task Force on US Strategy to Support Democracy and Counter Authoritarianism, *Reversing the Tide: Towards a New US Strategy to Support Democracy and Counter Authoritarianism* (Washington, DC: Freedom House, Center for Strategic and International Studies, and The McCain Institute, 2021), 5.

88 Samuel Huntington, "After 20 Years: The Future of the Third Wave," *Journal of Democracy* (1997): 5.

89 Larry Diamond, "Chasing Away the Democracy Blues," *Foreign Policy*, October 14, 2014.

90 US Department of State, "Memorandum From the Deputy Secretary of State (Clark) and the Under Secretary of State for Management (Kennedy) to Secretary of State Haig," October 26, 1981, https://history.state.gov/historicaldocuments/frus1981-88v41/d54.

91 US Department of State, "Memorandum From the Deputy Secretary of State (Clark) and the Under Secretary of State for Management (Kennedy) to Secretary of State Haig."

92 William Inboden, "Ronald Reagan Offers Hope That We Can Reverse the Decline of Democracy," *Washington Post*, December 6, 2022, https://www.washingtonpost.com/made-by-history/2022/12/06/democratic-decline-reagan/; Diamond, "Democracy's Arc," 18; and Huntington, *The Third Wave*, 13.

93 Maria J. Stephan, Sadaf Lakhani, and Nadia Naviwala, *Aid to Civil Society: A Movement Mindset* (Washington, DC: United States Institute for Peace, 2015).

94 Chenoweth and Stephan, *The Role of External Support in Nonviolent Campaigns*, 1.

95 Jaime Jackson, Jonathan Pinckney, and Miranda Rivers, *External Support for Nonviolent Action*, (Washington, DC: United States Institute for Peace, 2022), 37.

96 Chenoweth and Stephan, *The Role of External Support in Nonviolent Campaigns*, 72; and Jackson, Pinckney, and Rivers, *External Support for Nonviolent Action*, 37.

97 Chenoweth and Stephan, *The Role of External Support in Nonviolent Campaigns*, 80. Furthermore, just as coordination can strengthen movement support, lack of coordination among external actors, particularly in funding, may present liabilities to movements. See: Ben Naimark-Rowse, *Dollars and Dissent: Donor Support for Grassroots Organizing and Nonviolent Movements* (Washington, DC: ICNC Press, 2022), 46-48, 79-80.

98 In the study, "training" was defined as: "The provision of leadership training, organizational capacity-building, labor organizing, nonviolent action or movement training, legal training, and medical training. Note that this category explicitly requires the supporter to train the activists (not just provide space for training, which is coded as technical support)." See Chenoweth and Stephan, *The Role of External Support in Nonviolent Campaigns*, 15.

99 Chenoweth and Stephan, *The Role of External Support in Nonviolent Campaigns*, 67.

100 This paragraph draws from or uses language (with permission) from Ackerman and Merriman, *Preventing Mass Atrocities*, 13.

101 This paragraph draws from or uses language (with permission) from Ackerman and Merriman, *Preventing Mass Atrocities*, 24.

102 This paragraph draws from or uses language (with permission) from Ackerman and Merriman, *Preventing Mass Atrocities: From a Responsibility to Protect (RtoP) to a Right to Assist (RtoA) Campaigns of Civil Resistance* (Washington, DC: ICNC Press, 2019), 11-12.

103 Gene Sharp, *There Are Realistic Alternatives* (Boston: Albert Einstein Institution, 2003), 3; Hardy Merriman and Jack DuVall, "Dissolving Terrorism at Its Roots," in *Nonviolence: An Alternative for Countering Global Terror(ism)*, eds. Ralph Summy and Senthil Ram (Hauppauge, New York: Nova Science Publishers, 2007).

104 This paragraph draws from or uses language (with permission) from Ackerman and Merriman, *Preventing Mass Atrocities*, 12.

105 Erica Chenoweth, "People Are in the Streets Protesting Donald Trump. But When Does Protest Actually Work?," *Washington Post*, November 21, 2016, https://www.washingtonpost.com/news/monkey-cage/wp/2016/11/21/people-are-in-the-streets-protesting-donald-trump-but-when-does-protest-actually-work/.

106 Chenoweth and Stephan, *Why Civil Resistance Works*, 34-38.

107 This paragraph draws from or uses language (with permission) from Ackerman and Merriman, *Preventing Mass Atrocities*, 12.

108 This paragraph draws from or uses language (with permission) from Ackerman and Merriman, *Preventing Mass Atrocities*, 12.

109 This paragraph draws from or uses language (with permission) from Ackerman and Merriman, *Preventing Mass Atrocities*, 12.

110 This paragraph draws from or uses language (with permission) from Ackerman and Merriman, *Preventing Mass Atrocities*, 12.

111 Chenoweth and Stephan, *The Role of External Support in Nonviolent Campaigns*, 21.

112 Correlations of increased likelihood of defections and higher levels of women's participation are found in movements with 450,000 participants or more. See Erica Chenoweth, *Women's Participation and the Fate of Nonviolent Campaigns: A Report on the Women in Resistance (WIRE) Dataset* (Broomfield, Colorado: One Earth Future Foundation, 2019), 14-21.

113 Jonathan Pinckney and Miranda Rivers, *Precarity and Power: Reflections on Women and Youth in Nonviolent Action* (Washington, DC: United States Institute of Peace, 2021).

114 Charles Butcher, John Laidlaw Gray, and Liesel Mitchell, "Striking It Free? Organized Labor and the Outcomes of Civil Resistance," *Journal of Global Security Studies* (2018): 302-321.

115 Different groups of activists and organizers will have different profiles and initial needs in this regard. In some cases, a group seeking to start a movement may have internal unity and tight communal ties, but few bridging ties to other groups. For example, members of traditionally excluded minority groups that are based in a certain geographic portion of a country sometimes face these circumstances. In that case, the assets of the group are high levels of internal organization and unity, but the deficiency is their connections to other groups in society. Thus, potential coalition partners must be identified and approached so that relationships can be intentionally built—this may happen through a process of convening and dialogue, incorporating trusted intermediaries, and emphasizing common goals and shared aspects of identity (i.e., based on gender, class, or other aspects of identity). In other cases, movements originate from members of majority groups that have broad ties, but relatively weak unity of purpose and unity on leadership. Here, a group's strength is its potential to achieve broad mobilization, but its deficiencies are lack of organization and a lack of strong ties. The group then needs to increase its internal unity and significantly deepen is already broad relationships. Otherwise, it runs the risk of an external trigger event—i.e., price hikes on essential goods or a publicized incident of regime brutality—generating rapid mobilization that is quickly repressed and diminishes due to lack of strategic direction.

116 Doing so can both improve the movement's chance of success and reinforce a choice of nonviolent means. For example, when a tightly organized group believes that broader mobilization is impossible, it can lead that group to conclude that violence may be a better choice to achieve its goals. Thus, broadening social ties can also strengthen commitment to civil resistance. See Ches Thurber, "Social Ties and the Strategy of Civil Resistance," *International Studies Quarterly* (2019); and Marianne Dahl et al., "Accounting for Numbers: Group Characteristics and the Choice of Violent and Nonviolent Tactics," reviewed and pre-typeset manuscript (2021).

117 For example, researcher Stephen Feldstein finds that "companies based in liberal democracies (for example, Germany, France, Israel, Japan, South Korea, the United Kingdom, the United States) are actively selling sophisticated equipment to unsavory regimes." See Stephen Feldstein, "The Global Expansion of AI Surveillance," Carnegie Endowment for International Peace, September 2019.

118 "Smart" repression refers to repressive tactics that are less visible or less attributable to the regime, and thus less likely to generate domestic or international backlash.

119 Matthew Cebul and Jonathan Pinckney, *Digital Authoritarianism and Nonviolent Action: Challenging the Digital Counterrevolution* (Washington, DC: United States Institute of Peace, 2021).

120 For example, efforts to counter misinformation range from the Atlantic Council's Digital Forensic Research Lab to IREX's "Learn to Discern" programs in various countries.

121 Cebul and Pinckney, *Digital Authoritarianism and Nonviolent Action*, 18.

122 Ackerman and Merriman, *Preventing Mass Atrocities*, 13. Notably, movement training is not a onetime effort in the preorganizing phase: training support should be considered an ongoing need and process that takes place throughout all subsequent movement phases, and can be adapted to different needs within these phases.

123 In particular, direct financial support from a foreign state to a nonviolent campaign can be dangerous. Examining data on the issue, Evan Perkoski and Erica Chenoweth conclude that direct "foreign state support...can increase the likelihood of mass killings, even in the case of a nonviolent movement." See Perkoski and Chenoweth, *Nonviolent Resistance and Prevention of Mass Killings During Popular Uprisings*, ICNC Special Report Series 2 (2018): 18; and Ackerman and Merriman, *Preventing Mass Atrocities*, 13-4.

124 Chenoweth and Stephan, *The Role of External Support in Nonviolent Campaigns*, 3; and Naimark-Rowse, *Dollars and Dissent*, 46-48, 79-80.

125 This paragraph draws from or uses language (with permission) from Ackerman and Merriman, *Preventing Mass Atrocities*, 14.

126 Chenoweth and Stephan, *The Role of External Support in Nonviolent Campaigns*, 70.

127 Chenoweth and Stephan, *The Role of External Support in Nonviolent Campaigns*, 71.

128 Chenoweth and Stephan, *The Role of External Support in Nonviolent Campaigns*, 71.

129 A well-organized movement may choose to create its own trigger event. Ongoing evidence of authoritarian abuses offer regular opportunities for a movement to identify a flash point and control the timing of its initial public mobilization. However, trigger events may also be unanticipated.

130 This paragraph draws from or uses language (with permission) from Ackerman and Merriman, *Preventing Mass Atrocities*, 14.

131 Ackerman and Merriman, *Preventing Mass Atrocities*, 14.

132 Jonathan Pinckney, *Making or Breaking Nonviolent Discipline in Civil Resistance Movements* (Washington, DC: ICNC Press, 2016), 38.

133 Pinckney, *Making or Breaking Nonviolent Discipline*, 39.

134 See Chenoweth and Stephan, *Why Civil Resistance Works*; Perkoski and Chenoweth, *Nonviolent Resistance and Prevention*; and Chenoweth and Stephan, "Drop Your Weapons."

135 Chenoweth, "The Future of Nonviolent Resistance," 79.

136 Elizabeth Tompkins, "A Quantitative Reevaluation of Radical Flank Effects within Nonviolent Campaigns," *Research in Social Movements, Conflicts and Change* (2015), 103-135.

137 Omar Wasow, "Agenda Seeding: How 1960s Black Protests Moved Elites, Public Opinion and Voting," *American Political Science Review* (2020), 638-659; and Jordi Muño and Eva Anduiza, "'If a Fight Starts, Watch the Crowd': The Effect of Violence on Popular Support for Social Movements," *Journal of Peace Research* (2019): 485-498.

138 Emiliano Huet-Vaughn, "Quiet Riot: The Causal Effect of Protest Violence" (working paper, September 25, 2013).

139 Victor Asal et al., "Gender Ideologies and Forms of Contentious Mobilization in the Middle East," *Journal of Peace Research* (2013): 305-318.

140 Erica Chenoweth, "Backfire in Action: Insights from Nonviolent Campaigns, 1946-2006," in *The Paradox of Repression and Nonviolent Movements*, eds. Lester R. Kurtz and Lee A. Smithey (Syracuse, New York: Syracuse University Press, 2018), 28.

141 For those who may consider simultaneous support for both armed groups and nonviolent movements, research shows that such support "is correlated with lower [civil resistance movement] participation rates, lower chances of maintaining nonviolent discipline, lower chances of eliciting security force defections, and lower chances of movement success." See Chenoweth and Stephan, *The Role of External Support in Nonviolent Campaigns*, 2.

142 Erica Chenoweth, Andrew Hocking, and Zoe Marks, "A Dynamic Model of Nonviolent Resistance Strategy," *PLOS ONE* (2022), 1.

143 Chenoweth and Stephan, *Why Civil Resistance Works*, 58.

144 For example, see Anika L. Binnendijk and Ivan Marovic, "Power and Persuasion: Nonviolent Strategies to Influence State Security Forces in Serbia (2000) and Ukraine (2004)," *Communist and Post-Communist Studies* 39, no. 3, Special Issue: Democratic Revolutions in Post-Communist States (2006): 411-429.

145 See Dennis Blair, *Military Engagement Influencing Armed Forces Worldwide to Support Democratic Transitions*, Vol. I (Washington, DC: Brookings Institution, 2013).

146 This paragraph draws from or uses language (with permission) from Ackerman and Merriman, *Preventing Mass Atrocities*, 16-17.

147 Chenoweth and Stephan, "Drop Your Weapons."

148 Jonathan Pinckney, *How to Win Well: Civil Resistance Breakthroughs and the Path to Democracy* (Washington, DC: ICNC Press, 2021), 6-7.

149 Pinckney, *How to Win Well*, 8-14; and Marianne Dahl and Kristian Skrede Gleditsch, "Clouds with Silver Linings: How Mobilization Shapes the Impact of Coups on Democratization," *European Journal of International Relations* (2023). As Dahl and Gleditsch note, coups that take place amid popular nonviolent mobilization are more likely to lead to democratic outcomes than coups that take place in the absence of popular nonviolent mobilization.

150 Pinckney, *How to Win Well*, 19-20.

151 Ackerman and Merriman, *Preventing Mass Atrocities*, 17.

152 Pinckney, *When Civil Resistance Succeeds*; and Pinckney, *From Dissent to Democracy*.

153 Tom Ginsburg, "How Authoritarians Use International Law," *Journal of Democracy* (2020): 55-56.

154 Embedding this norm within the UN system would allow it to languish under authoritarian vetoes.

155 For example, see Ash Jain and Matthew Kroenig, with Tobias Bunde, Sophia Gaston, and Yuichi Hosoya, "From the G7 to a D-10: Strengthening Democratic Cooperation for Today's Challenges," Atlantic Council, 2021; and Ash Jain, Matthew Kroenig, and Jonas Parello-Plesner, "An Alliance of Democracies: From Concept to Reality in an Era of Strategic Competition," Atlantic Council and Alliance of Democracies, 2021.

156 Such treaties include: the International Convention on Civil and Political Rights (ICCPR), the African Charter on Human and Peoples' Rights, the European Convention on Human Rights and Fundamental Freedoms (ECHR), the American Convention on Human Rights, and the Convention on the Elimination of All Forms of Racial Discrimination. UN General Assembly resolutions include the Universal Declaration of Human Rights, and the Declaration on the Right and Responsibility of Individuals, Groups and Organs of Society to Promote and Protect Universally Recognized Human Rights and Fundamental Freedoms (Declaration on Human Rights Defenders). International institutions include the Human Rights Committee, the UN Human Rights Council, and the International Labour Organization. See Elizabeth Wilson, "International Legal Basis of Support for Nonviolent Activists and Movements," in *Is Authoritarianism Staging a Comeback?*, eds. Matthew Burrows and Maria J. Stephan (Washington, DC: Atlantic Council, 2015).

157 For a full list, see UN Office of the High Commissioner for Human Rights (OHCHR), Commentary to the Declaration on the Right and Responsibility of Individuals, Groups and Organs of Society to Promote and Protect Universally Recognized Human Rights and Fundamental Freedoms, July 2011, accessed January 7, 2023, https://www.refworld.org/docid/4e2fc3f02.html.

158 ICCPR, article 22(1).

159 Freedom of association "involves the right of individuals to interact and organize among themselves to collectively express, promote, pursue and defend common interests." Furthermore, the forms of association covered are broad: "Religious societies, political parties, commercial undertakings and trade unions are as protected by article 22 as are cultural or human rights organizations, soccer clubs or associations of stamp collectors." Moreover, such associations need not be legally registered, and instead may be *de facto* associations. See Hina Jilani, "Report of the Special Representative of the Secretary-General on Human Rights Defenders, Hina Jilani," UN General Assembly, A/59/401, para. 46; and Margaret Sekaggya, "Report of the Special Rapporteur on the Situation of Human Rights Defenders," UN General Assembly, A/64/226, para. 20.

160 Maina Kiai, "Report of the Special Rapporteur on the Rights to Freedom of Peaceful Assembly and of Association," UN General Assembly, A/HRC/23/39, para. 8.

161 Kiai, "Report of the Special Rapporteur on the Rights to Freedom of Peaceful Assembly and of Association," para. 10.

162 In addition, grounds for a right to assistance can also sometimes be found in regional commitments (i.e., the Council of Europe Recommendations on the Legal Status of NGOs), and bilateral investment treaties, such as US treaties with Kazakhstan and Kyrgyzstan, which "expressly extend investment-treaty protections to organizations not 'organized for pecuniary gain.' The letters from the White House transmitting these treaties to the U.S. Senate explicitly state that they cover 'charitable and non-profit entities.'" See Rutzen, "Civil Society Under Assault," 34. For deeper investigation of bilateral treaty protections for civil society organizations, see "International Investment Treaty Protection of Not-for-Profit Organizations," (working paper), Regional NGO Law Rapid-Response Mechanism, May 2008 update.

163 Declaration on the Elimination of All Forms of Intolerance and of Discrimination Based on Religion or Belief, Article 6, 6(f), as cited in Kiai, "Report of the Special Rapporteur on the Rights to Freedom of Peaceful Assembly and of Association," para. 15.

164 UN Human Rights Committee, communication No. 1274/2004, *Korneenko et al. v. Belarus*, views adopted on October 31, 2006, para. 7.2., as cited in Kiai, "Report of the Special Rapporteur on the Rights to Freedom of Peaceful Assembly and of Association," para. 16.

165 "Protecting Human Rights Defenders," A/HRC/RES/22/6*, as cited in Kiai, "Report of the Special Rapporteur on the Rights to Freedom of Peaceful Assembly and of Association," para. 15.

166 "Declaration on the Right and Responsibility of Individuals, Groups and Organs of Society to Promote and Protect Universally Recognized Human Rights and Fundamental Freedoms," A/RES/53/144, as cited in Kiai, "Report of the Special Rapporteur on the Rights to Freedom of Peaceful Assembly and of Association," para. 17.

167 ICCPR, article 22(2).

168 Kiai, "Report of the Special Rapporteur on the Rights to Freedom of Peaceful Assembly and of Association," para. 19; Rutzen, "Civil Society Under Assault," 34; and Voule, "Report of the Special Rapporteur on the rights to freedom of peaceful assembly and of association, Clément Nyaletsossi Voule," A/HRC/50/23, para. 14.

169 One criterion to evaluate the legitimacy of a particular restriction to civil society would be to evaluate it in light of "sectoral equity." As the Community of Democracies and Maina Kiai, former UN Special Rapporteur on Freedom of Peaceful Assembly and of Freedom of Association, note: "Governments must refrain from adopting measures that disproportionately target or burden civil society organizations (CSOs), such as imposing onerous vetting rules, procedures, or other CSO-specific requirements not applied to the corporate sector....[For example,] commercial companies have been...used for terrorist or money-laundering purposes, so that the 'protection against terrorism and prevention of money laundering' cannot be seen as a legitimate ground for discrimination between the treatment of CSOs and the corporate sector." See Kiai, "Report of the Special Rapporteur on the Rights to Freedom of Peaceful Assembly and of Association," para. 24.

170 Kiai, "Report of the Special Rapporteur on the Rights to Freedom of Peaceful Assembly and of Association," paras. 27, 30, 32.

171   Kiai, "Report of the Special Rapporteur on the Rights to Freedom of Peaceful Assembly and of Association," para. 36.

172   For example, see: Anthony H. Cordesman, "Russia and the 'Color Revolution," Center for Strategic and International Studies (CSIS), May 28, 2014.
https://www.csis.org/analysis/russia-and-color-revolution; Stella Chen. "China's top police chief warns law enforcement to stay alert to risk of 'colour revolution' ahead of major Communist Party gathering," South China Morning Post, September 18, 2022. https://www.scmp.com/news/china/politics/article/3192868/chinas-top-police-chief-warns-law-enforcement-stay-alert-risk

173   Wilson, "International Legal Basis of Support," 160. In a subsequent work, Wilson lists rights from the ICCPR that "a movement can invoke and exercise while waging their nonviolent struggle," including:
Collective rights
    Article 1 (self-determination)
Expressive and associational rights
    Article 18 (freedom of thought, conscience, and religions)
    Article 19 (freedom of opinion and expression)
    Article 21 (freedom of peaceful assembly)
    Article 22 (freedom of association)
    Article 25 (right to political participation)
Bodily integrity rights
    Article 6 (right to life)Article 7 (freedom from torture; cruel, inhuman and degrading treatment)
    Article 9 (liberty and security; freedom from arbitrary arrest and detention)
    Article 10 (dignity)
See Elizabeth A. Wilson, *People Power Movements and International Human Rights: Creating a Legal Framework*, (Washington, DC: ICNC Press, 2017), 66.

174   "Report of the United Nations High Commissioner on Human Rights, Seminar on Effective Measures and Best Practices to Ensure the Promotion and Protection of Human Rights in the Context of Peaceful Protests," UN General Assembly Document A/HRC/25/32/, para. 11; the seminar took place on December 2, 2013.

175   Wilson, "International Legal Basis of Support," 159-60.

176   ICCPR, Art. 21.

177   "General Comment No. 37 (2020) on the Right of Peaceful Assembly (Article 21)," Human Rights Committee, CCPR/C/GC/37, September 17, 2020, paras. 15-20; and Kiai, "Report of the Special Rapporteur on the Rights to Freedom of Peaceful Assembly and of Association," paras. 49, 78.

178   This paragraph draws from or uses language (with permission) from Ackerman and Merriman, *Preventing Mass Atrocities*, 28. Also see Peter Ackerman and Michael Glennon, "The Right Side of the Law," *American Interest* (September 1, 2007).

179   This paragraph draws from or uses language (with permission) from Ackerman and Merriman, *Preventing Mass Atrocities*, 28.

180   This paragraph draws from or uses language (with permission) from Ackerman and Merriman, *Preventing Mass Atrocities*, 28.

181   ICCPR, Article 1(1).

182   ICCPR, Article 25.

183   Ackerman and Merriman, *Preventing Mass Atrocities*, 29.

184   Michael Ignatieff, "The Return of Sovereignty," review of *Sovereign Equality and Moral Disagreement*,by Brad R. Roth, *New Republic*, January 25, 2012,
https://newrepublic.com/article/100040/sovereign-equality-moral-disagreement-government-roth.

185   For a discussion of how the AU implicitly factors movements into government recognition decisions, see Florian Kriener and Elizabeth A. Wilson, "The Rise of Nonviolent Protest Movements and the African Union's Legal Framework," *ESIL Reflections* (2021); and for a discussion of criteria by which a movement may be recognized under international law, see Elizabeth A. Wilson, "'People Power' and the Problem of Sovereignty in International Law," *Duke Journal of Comparative & International Law* 26 (2016): 551-594.

186   Wilson, "'People Power' and the Problem of Sovereignty in International Law," 593-594.

187   Based on World Bank data, 2021.

188   For example, see Jain et. al., "From the G7 to a D-10"; and Jain, Kroenig, and Parello-Plesner, "An Alliance of Democracies.".

189   See Anders Fogh Rasmussen and Ivo Daalder, "Memo on an Economic Article 5 to Counter Authoritarian Coercion," Chicago Council on Global Affairs and the Alliance of Democracies, June 2022; and Ash Jain and Matthew Kroenig, with Marianne Schneider-Petsinger, "A Democratic Trade Partnership: Ally Shoring to Counter Coercion and Secure Supply Chains," Atlantic Council, 2022.

190   For example, the Varieties of Democracy (V-Dem) project has developed its *Case for Democracy* policy brief series showing the benefits of democracy in areas such as peace, economic growth, education, responding to climate change, public health, service provision, transparency, and social protection for traditionally excluded groups; see these papers, https://www.v-dem.net/our-work/policy-collaborations/case-for-democracy/.

191   Jon Temin, "Civil Society Should Be at the Center of Foreign Policy," *Lawfare* (blog), Lawfare Institute in collaboration with the Brookings Institution, March 1, 2021,
https://www.lawfareblog.com/civil-society-should-be-center-foreign-policy.

192   Chenoweth, "Backfire in Action," 30.

193   Jackson, Pinckney, and Rivers, *External Support for Nonviolent Action*, 12; also see Sharon Nepstad, "Creating Transnational Solidarity: The Use of Narrative in the U.S.-Central America Peace Movement," *Mobilization: An International Quarterly* (2006), 21-36; and Christine Mason, "Women, Violence, and Nonviolent Resistance in East Timor," *Journal of Peace Research* (2005), 737-49.

194 Backfire occurs when repression imposes significant costs on the regime. Domestically, this can take the form of heightened movement support and mobilization, and/or defections from a regime's pillars of support. Internationally, backfire can happen through sanctions or withdrawal of foreign government support.

195 In this cited study, international backfire was defined as "economic sanctions by world or regional powers, or arms embargoes being put in place as a result of repressive violence against unarmed protests," but did not consider withdrawal of foreign support. See Jonathan Sutton, Charles R. Butcher, and Isak Svensson, "Explaining Political Jiu-jitsu: Institution-building and the Outcomes of Regime Violence against Unarmed Protests," *Journal of Peace Research* (2014), 564, 568.

196 Chenoweth, "Backfire in Action," 31.

197 Chenoweth and Stephan, *The Role of External Support in Nonviolent Campaigns*, 2.

198 Chenoweth and Stephan, *The Role of External Support in Nonviolent Campaigns*, 46.

199 Julia Grauvogel, Amanda A. Licht, and Christian von Soest, "Sanctions and Signals: How International Sanction Threats Trigger Domestic Protest in Targeted Regimes," *International Studies Quarterly* (2017): 86.

200 Chenoweth and Stephan, *Why Civil Resistance Works*, 27.

201 Dursun Peksen, and A. Cooper Drury, "Coercive or Corrosive: The Negative Impact of Economic Sanctions on Democracy," *International Interactions* (2010).

202 To address the scapegoating opportunity that broad sanctions offer to authoritarian elites, democracies may wish to couple these sanctions with "information campaigns explaining the rationale, mechanisms and objectives of their penalties." Agathe Demarais, "Why Sanctions Don't Work Against Dictatorships," *Journal of Democracy*, November 2022, https://www.journalofdemocracy.org/why-sanctions-dont-work-against-dictatorships/.

203 Chenoweth and Stephan, *The Role of External Support in Nonviolent Campaigns*, 76.

204 Named after lawyer Sergei Magnitsky, who was investigating corruption in Russia and died mysteriously while in jail, Magnitsky laws have been passed in a variety of countries and allow states to freeze assets and ban the travel of sanctioned individuals and entities.

205 *Multilateral Magnitsky Sanctions at Five Years*, Report of Human Rights First, Open Society Foundations, Raoul Wallenberg Centre for Human Rights, and Redress, November 2022, 5.

206 *Multilateral Magnitsky Sanctions at Five Years*, 5.

207 *Multilateral Magnitsky Sanctions at Five Years*, 5.

208 Eugenia Andreyuk and Anonymous, International Mechanisms for Accountability for Human Rights Violations in Belarus, German Marshall Fund, January 2022

209 Ibid.

210 US Department of Defense Directive 5205.82; also see a comprehensive set of essays on SSR and DIB in *Effective, Legitimate, Secure: Insights for Defense Institution Building*, eds. Alexandra Kerr and Michael Miklaucic (Washington, DC: Center for Complex Operations, Institute for National Strategic Studies, National Defense University, 2017).

211 Blair, *Military Engagement Influencing Armed Forces Worldwide to Support Democratic Transitions*, Vol. I, 11-12.

212 Blair, *Military Engagement Influencing Armed Forces Worldwide to Support Democratic Transitions*, Vol. I, 12.

213 The International Republican Institute (IRI) has written extensively on this topic. For example, see "Coercion, Capture, and Censorship: Case Studies on the CCP's Quest for Global Influence," IRI, 2022; "Global Thought Work—Case Studies on PRC Influence in Africa's Information Space," IRI, 2022; and "A World Safe for the Party: China's Authoritarian Influence and the Democratic Response," IRI, 2021.

214 "Coercion, Capture, and Censorship"; "Global Thought Work"; and "A World Safe for the Party."

215 For possible criteria to determine the nonviolent character of a movement, see page 47.

216 For a legal discussion, see Danny Auron, "The Derecognition Approach: Government, Illegality, Recognition, and Non-Violent Regime Change," *George Washington International Law Review* (2013), 443-499.

217 As Danny Auron writes: "Ultimately, if states have been unwilling to predicate recognition of new governments on non-compliance with internal legal norms in extra-territorial situations, why should continued governmental recognition not be predicated on similar requirements of avoiding international wrongs?" See Auron, "The Derecognition Approach," 495.

218 This subsection draws from or uses language (with permission) from Ackerman and Merriman, *Preventing Mass Atrocities*, 22-23.

219 This subsection draws from or uses language (with permission) from Ackerman and Merriman, *Preventing Mass Atrocities*, 23-25.

220 This subsection draws from or uses language (with permission) from Ackerman and Merriman, *Preventing Mass Atrocities*, 25-26.

221 Chenoweth and Stephan, *Why Civil Resistance Works*, 217.

222 Stephan, Lakhani, and Naviwala, Aid to Civil Society, 11.

Atlantic Council | Board of Directors

CHAIRMAN
*John F.W. Rogers

EXECUTIVE CHAIRMAN EMERITUS
*James L. Jones

PRESIDENT AND CEO
*Frederick Kempe

EXECUTIVE VICE CHAIRS
*Adrienne Arsht
*Stephen J. Hadley

VICE CHAIRS
*Robert J. Abernethy
*C. Boyden Gray
*Alexander V. Mirtchev

TREASURER
*George Lund

DIRECTORS
Todd Achilles
Timothy D. Adams
*Michael Andersson
David D. Aufhauser
Barbara Barrett
Colleen Bell
Stephen Biegun
Linden P. Blue
Adam Boehler
John Bonsell
Philip M. Breedlove
Richard R. Burt
*Teresa Carlson
*James E. Cartwright
John E. Chapoton
Ahmed Charai
Melanie Chen
Michael Chertoff
*George Chopivsky
Wesley K. Clark
*Helima Croft
*Ankit N. Desai
Dario Deste
Lawrence Di Rita
*Paula J. Dobriansky
Joseph F. Dunford, Jr.
Richard Edelman
Thomas J. Egan, Jr.
Stuart E. Eizenstat
Mark T. Esper
*Michael Fisch
Alan H. Fleischmann
Jendayi E. Frazer
Meg Gentle

Thomas H. Glocer
John B. Goodman
*Sherri W. Goodman
Jarosław Grzesiak
Murathan Günal
Michael V. Hayden
Tim Holt
*Karl V. Hopkins
Kay Bailey Hutchison
Ian Ihnatowycz
Mark Isakowitz
Wolfgang F. Ischinger
Deborah Lee James
*Joia M. Johnson
*Safi Kalo
Andre Kelleners
Brian L. Kelly
Henry A. Kissinger
John E. Klein
*C. Jeffrey Knittel
Joseph Konzelmann
Franklin D. Kramer
Laura Lane
Almar Latour
Yann Le Pallec
Jan M. Lodal
Douglas Lute
Jane Holl Lute
William J. Lynn
Mark Machin
Marco Margheri
Michael Margolis
Chris Marlin
William Marron
Christian Marrone
Gerardo Mato
Erin McGrain
John M. McHugh
*Judith A. Miller
Dariusz Mioduski
Michael J. Morell
*Richard Morningstar
Georgette Mosbacher
Majida Mourad
Virginia A. Mulberger
Mary Claire Murphy
Edward J. Newberry
Franco Nuschese
Joseph S. Nye
Ahmet M. Ören
Sally A. Painter
Ana I. Palacio
*Kostas Pantazopoulos
Alan Pellegrini
David H. Petraeus
*Lisa Pollina
Daniel B. Poneman

*Dina H. Powell McCormick
Michael Punke
Ashraf Qazi
Thomas J. Ridge
Gary Rieschel
Michael J. Rogers
Charles O. Rossotti
Harry Sachinis
C. Michael Scaparrotti
Ivan A. Schlager
Rajiv Shah
Gregg Sherrill
Jeff Shockey
Ali Jehangir Siddiqui
Kris Singh
Walter Slocombe
Christopher Smith
Clifford M. Sobel
James G. Stavridis
Michael S. Steele
Richard J.A. Steele
Mary Streett
*Gil Tenzer
*Frances F. Townsend
Clyde C. Tuggle
Melanne Verveer
Charles F. Wald
Michael F. Walsh
Ronald Weiser
*Al Williams
Maciej Witucki
Neal S. Wolin
*Jenny Wood
Guang Yang
Mary C. Yates
Dov S. Zakheim

HONORARY DIRECTORS
James A. Baker, III
Robert M. Gates
James N. Mattis
Michael G. Mullen
Leon E. Panetta
William J. Perry
Condoleezza Rice
Horst Teltschik
William H. Webster

Executive Committee Members

List as of March 6, 2023

www.ingramcontent.com/pod-product-compliance
Lightning Source LLC
Chambersburg PA
CBHW042348030426
42335CB00031B/3500